JUST TEN YEARS AGO, the first Rand Mc-Nally Pocket World Atlas was published. It was the most ambitious and costly project undertaken up to that time in the field of paper-bound book publishing—a joint venture of the two largest firms in their respective fields. It was a wonderful reference work, an extraordinary value, and enjoyed very large sales.

NOW THAT BOOK has been completely remade and enlarged. This new edition is almost thirty per cent bigger than the original. All the maps are new—both color and black and white. All the tables and charts of geographic, economic and political information are new. And the index is not only new but very much more detailed. Even the binding has been done by a new and very superior process.

There is truly no comparable reference work in a low-priced, paperback edition.

THE NEW
Rand McNally
POCKET
WORLD
ATLAS

POCKET BOOKS, INC. • NEW YORK

THE NEW RAND McNALLY POCKET WORLD ATLAS

A *Giant Cardinal* edition

1st printing..........September, 1951
12th printing..........February, 1963

The boundaries shown for certain countries in Europe and
Asia, in this atlas, are based upon de facto situations resulting
from war or revolution. In some cases, the boundaries
have been established by agreement pending final peace
treaties. The de facto boundaries shown do not necessarily
reflect moral or diplomatic approval by either publisher
or government. This statement applies, in particular, to
Germany, Poland, the Soviet Union, China and Japan.

This original *Giant Cardinal*** edition is printed from brand-new plates
made from newly set, clear, easy-to-read type.
Giant Cardinal editions are published by Pocket Books, Inc., and
are printed and distributed in the U.S.A. by Affiliated Publishers,
a division of Pocket Books, Inc., 630 Fifth Avenue, New York 20, N.Y.
*Trademark registered in the United States and other countries.
**Trademark of Pocket Books, Inc., 630 Fifth
Avenue, New York 20, N.Y., in the United States
and other countries.

L

Copyright, ©, 1961, by Rand McNally & Company. Copyright, ©,
1961, under International Copyright Union by Rand McNally
& Company. All rights reserved. This *Giant Cardinal* edition
is published by arrangement with Rand McNally & Company.
Printed in the U.S.A.

CONTENTS

THE WORLD IN MAPS

HOW TO USE THIS WORLD ATLAS

The Rand McNally-Pocket WORLD ATLAS contains a selection of up-to-date maps covering 169 pages, designed to provide complete coverage of the mid-twentieth-century world. From the air-age Polar Map of the World at the beginning to the reference map of the Yukon at the end, this authoritative little ATLAS presents accurate, detailed maps of all major divisions of the world and of the United States.

A handy-size, reference atlas should be the constant companion of every traveler, reader, radio listener, and television viewer; for the map is a magic eye which enables one to see beyond the limited horizons of personal experience and thus bring into focus the whole wide world.

We turn to a map when we want to see where we are, where we have been, where we are going, how far it is, what lies in between, and the many other geographical understandings that a traveler or reader needs to have. Most of us must picture the world in our minds, however, rather than see it in person. The indispensable means to this end is an ever ready atlas of convenient size.

HOW TO FIND THE MAP YOU NEED

Three separate reference aids are provided to help you find the right map at the right time. First, there is the Table of Contents on pages 5-6, which gives the titles of the maps in order of sequence from pages 33 to 201. Second, on pages 10-27, is the Gazetteer-Index of the World, which lists in alphabetical order, and with page and map-location references, every important political division of the world. Third, at the end of the volume is an index of selected cities and towns, also with page and map-location references.

Thus, to find a specific continent, country, or state map, turn to the Table of Contents; for any political division, large or small, turn to the alphabetical Gazetteer-Index; and for any important city, turn to the main Index.

BASIC FACTS OBTAINABLE FROM MAPS

To the person who has learned to "read" rather than just "look at" maps, every reference to the Rand McNally-Pocket WORLD ATLAS can be made a source of richer geographical knowledge. For instance, suppose you are interested primarily in locating Berlin in Germany. Your city Index tells you to look on page 45 for the best map. Having found the city you are looking for in key section B6, see what interesting facts are revealed about its national, continental, and world location from this and other maps. How far is it from Berlin to Vienna? From Berlin to Trieste? The scale of 109 miles to one inch will give you one set of answers, and the bar scale can be used for checking. How far is it from the Baltic Sea to Berlin? From the Kiel Canal? From the Swiss border?

How does Germany compare in size with other countries of Europe? To answer this you can turn to the map of Europe on pages 36-37 and compare Germany by eye with Spain, Yugoslavia, or any other country shown. Such comparisons are reliable on the conic projection used, since this is a small-scale map covering a large area. Or, if you compare Germany, on pages 44-45, with France, on pages 42-43, your visual impression of comparative size is reliable, since both of these maps are on the same scale. To check your impression, turn to the statistical facts of area given for each country in the Gazetteer-Index.

HOW TO FIND PLACES ON THE MAPS

Both the Gazetteer-Index and the main Index of cities and towns provide map-location references for every item in the form of key letters and numbers. Each letter represents an east-west strip across the map bounded by two parallels. Each number represents a north-south strip bounded by two meridians. The complete key, or combination of letter and number, enables one to find the zone or area formed by the intersection of the two strips on the map. Thus, Seoul at H3 on page 67, is located by following strip H across the map until it intersects with strip 3, and then finding the name and symbol of the city within the zone of intersection.

Two or three hints or cautions will be helpful. Note that on some maps of large areas, such as the continents, the lines of latitude and longutude are both curved. Therefore the east-west and north-south strips will be similarly curved, and the key letters and numbers will

be located differently from the usual pattern. As an example, see the map of Eurasia, pages 62-63.

Another point to watch for in locating cities is to find the symbol as well as the name. In some cases the symbol is in one key zone, while the name is mostly or entirely in another. The key references to cities and towns are always to the symbols rather than to the names. The key references to countries and other area names, however, are usually to the zone in which the first letters of the name appear.

HOW TO DETERMINE THE RELATIVE IMPORTANCE OF CITIES

From three to five sizes of type are used in the maps of the Rand McNally-Pocket WORLD ATLAS to show comparative sizes of cities and towns. For example, on the map of Western Europe, London, Paris, and Berlin are all in the largest size of type used for city names. Liverpool, Marseilles, and Leipzig are in slightly smaller type to show that they are of less importance than the three great capitals, but comparable in size and importance to each other. Plymouth, Bordeaux, and Lübeck are classed in a third group by still smaller type.

In general, maps on the same scale, or approximately the same, have the same breakdown for population classifications; but no one fixed set of groups could be made applicable to all maps. After the name of each city in the Index, however, the latest official population figure will be found. All figures for cities of the United States are from the 1960 census.

THE SPELLING OF GEOGRAPHICAL NAMES

In general, the Rand McNally-Pocket WORLD ATLAS follows the rules and decisions of the United States Board on Geographic Names in the spellings that are used. Where more than one spelling is currently in use for names in the United States, the authority followed has been the United States Postal Guide. Foreign city names are usually spelled just as they are in the local language whenever that language uses the Latin alphabet. Capitals of countries, however, are spelled according to conventional English usage, with the local form, if different, given in parentheses.

Region or Political Division	Capital	Population Estimated 1/1/1960‡	Area in sq. miles
Aden..............	Aden	147,000	80
Aden [Protectorate]............	Aden, Aden Colony	671,000	105,000
Afghanistan†............	Kabul	13,310,000	250,000
Africa................	....	233,718,700	11,635,000
Alabama..............	Montgomery	3,266,740	51,609
Alaska................	Juneau	226,167	586,400
Albania†..............	Tiranē	1,562,000	11,100
Alberta...............	Edmonton	1,268,000	255,285
Algeria...............	Algiers (Alger)	10,003,000	80,938
Andaman & Nicobar Is.	Port Blair	39,000	3,143
Andorra..............	Andorra	6,500	175
Angola...............	Luanda	4,496,000	481,350
Antarctica.............	....	....	5,100,000
Antigua (incl. Barbuda)........	St. John's	58,000	171
Arabian Peninsula...........	....	12,102,000	900,000
Argentina†.............	Buenos Aires	20,737,000	1,084,359
Arizona...............	Phoenix	1,302,161	113,909
Arkansas..............	Little Rock	1,786,272	53,104
Armenia (S.S.R.)...........	Yerevan	1,812,000	11,590
Aruba................	Oranjestad	80,500	68
Ascension I.............	Georgetown	220	34
Asia.................	....	1,691,327,800	17,035,000
Australia†.............	Canberra	10,050,000	2,974,581
Australian Capital Territory.....	Canberra	37,000	939
Austria†..............	Vienna (Wien)	7,082,000	32,374
Azerbaidzhan (S.S.R.)........	Baku	3,727,000	33,440
Azores Is..............	....	342,000	890
Bahamas..............	Nassau	136,000	4,404
Bahrain...............	Manama	129,000	231
Balearic Is..............	Palma	475,000	1,936
Barbados..............	Bridgetown	241,000	166
Basutoland.............	Maseru	742,000	11,716
Bechuanaland...........	Mafeking, S. Afr.	368,000	275,000
Belgium†..............	Brussels (Bruxelles)	9,117,000	11,779
Bermuda..............	Hamilton	46,000	22
Bhutan...............	Punakha	670,000	19,500
Bismarck Archipelago........	....	172,000	19,200
Bolivia†...............	La Paz, Sucre	3,366,000	424,162
Borneo, Indonesian........	....	3,800,000	208,286
Brazil†...............	Brasília	64,837,000	3,288,042
British Columbia..........	Victoria	1,594,000	366,255
British Commonwealth of Nations.................	London	641,951,400	12,406,518
British Guiana............	Georgetown	558,000	82,997
British Honduras..........	Belize	91,000	8,867
Brunei................	Brunei	81,000	2,226
Bulgaria†..............	Sofia (Sofiya)	7,859,000	42,796
Burma†................	Rangoon	20,303,000	261,610

† *Member of the United Nations (1960).* * *Not shown on map.*

INDEX OF THE WORLD

Region or Political Division	Form of Government and Ruling Power	Index Key	Map Page
Aden....................	Colony (Br.)	H7	63
Aden [Protectorate].........	Protectorates (Br.)	H7	81
Afghanistan†..............	Kingdom	B3	73
Africa....................	....	......	77
Alabama..................	State (U.S.)	......	105
Alaska...................	State (U.S.)	......	104
Albania†..................	People's Republic	B2	59
Alberta...................	Province (Canada)	C6	191
Algeria...................	Departments (France)	C6	77
Andaman & Nicobar Is.......	Territory (India)	F9	73
Andorra..................	Principality	A6	47
Angola...................	Overseas Province (Portugal)	C3	83
Antarctica................		L3	35
Antigua (incl. Barbuda).......	Territory, West Indies Federation	n16	99
Arabian Peninsula..........	....	......	63
Argentina†................	Federal Republic	......	87, 91
Arizona..................	State (U.S.)	......	107
Arkansas.................	State (U.S.)	......	108
Armenia (S.S.R.)...........	Soviet Socialist Republic (Sov. Un.)	E7	61
Aruba...................	Division of Neth. Antilles (Neth.)	*B4	87
Ascension I...............	Dependency (St. Helena, Br.)	G4	77
Asia†....................	....	......	63
Australia†.................	Fed. Commonwealth (Comm. of Nat.)	......	85
Australian Capital Territory..	Federal Territory (Australia)	G8	85
Austria†..................	Federal Republic	E6	45
Azerbaidzhan (S.S.R.).......	Soviet Socialist Republic (Sov. Un.)	E7	61
Azores Is.................	Overseas Provinces (Portugal)	C3	77
Bahamas..................	Colony (Br.)	B5	99
Bahrain..................	Sheikdom (Br. protection)	C8	81
Balearic Is................	Province (Spain)	C7	47
Barbados.................	Territory, West Indies Federation	p17	99
Basutoland...............	Prot. Territory (Br.)	I8	77
Bechuanaland..............	Prot. (Br.)	I8	77
Belgium†.................	Kingdom	B6	43
Bermuda.................	Colony (Br.)	D16	35
Bhutan..................	Principality (Indian protection)	C9	73
Bismarck Archipelago.......	Districts (N. Gui. Ter., Austl. Tr.)	h12	85
Bolivia†..................	Republic	E4	87
Borneo, Indonesian.........	Province (Indonesia)	E4	69
Brazil†...................	Federal Republic	......	87, 89
British Columbia...........	Province (Canada)	......	191
British Commonwealth of Nations...............	Free Association	......	......
British Guiana.............	Colony (Br.)	C5	87
British Honduras...........	Colony (Br.)	B3	95
Brunei...................	Protected Sultanate (Br.)	E4	69
Bulgaria†.................	People's Republic	D7	51
Burma†..................	Republic	D10	73

‡Census of April 1, 1960 for U.S. states and possessions.

11

Region or Political Division	Capital	Population Estimated 1/1/1960‡	Area in sq. miles
California...................	Sacramento	15,717,204	158,693
Cambodia†.................	Phnom Penh	5,056,000	53,650
Cameroun..................	Yaoundé	4,129,000	183,333
Canada†...................	Ottawa	17,678,000	3,851,809
Canal Zone................	Balboa Heights	60,000	553
Canary Is..................		879,000	2,808
Cape of Good Hope..........	Capetown	4,893,000	278,839
Cape Verde Is..............	Praia	193,000	1,557
Caroline Is................		48,000	461
Cayman Is.................	Georgetown	8,000	93
Celebes....................		6,371,000	72,986
Central African Republic†......	Bangui	1,224,000	227,118
Central America............		10,929,000	208,269
Ceylon†...................	Colombo	9,643,000	25,332
Chad, Republic of †..........	Fort Lamy	2,612,000	466,640
Channel Is.................		101,000	75
Chile†....................	Santiago	7,560,000	286,396
China (excl. Formosa)..........	Peking (Peiping)	699,966,000	3,900,000
Colombia†.................	Bogotá	14,105,000	439,519
Colorado..................	Denver	1,753,947	104,247
Comoro Is.................	Dzaoudzi	183,000	834
Congo (Rep. of Congo Capital: Brazzaville)†........	Brazzaville	816,000	125,890
Congo, The (Rep. of The Congo; Capital: Léopoldville)†........	Léopoldville	13,732,000	905,329
Connecticut................	Hartford	2,535,234	5,009
Cook Is...................	Avarua (Rarotonga)	18,000	99
Corsica...................	Ajaccio	282,000	3,367
Costa Rica†................	San José	1,194,000	19,647
Crete.....................		500,000	3,235
Cuba†....................	Havana (Habana)	6,627,000	44,218
Curacao...................	Willemstad	127,500	174
Cyprus†...................	Nicosia	559,000	3,572
Czechoslovakia†.............	Prague (Praha)	13,639,000	49,354
Dahomey, Republic of†........	Porto-Novo	1,750,000	43,800
Delaware..................	Dover	446,292	2,057
Denmark†.................	Copenhagen (Köbenhavn)	4,580,000	16,576
District of Columbia...........	Washington	763,956	69
Dominica..................	Roseau	67,300	304
Dominican Republic†..........	Ciudad Trujillo	2,929,000	18,816
Easter I...................		650	46
Ecuador†..................	Quito	4,191,000	106,000
Egypt (U.A.R.).............	Cairo (El Qahira)	25,313,000	386,000
England & Wales...........	London	51,941,000	58,343
Eritrea....................	Asmara	1,587,000	46,000

Region or Political Division	Form of Government and Ruling Power	Index Key	Map Page
California...............	State (U.S.)	......	111,113
Cambodia†...............	Kingdom	F5	71
Cameroun...............	Republic (Fr. Com.)	F7	77
Canada†................	Federal State (Comm. of Nat.)		101
Canal Zone..............	Possession (U.S.)	k11	95
Canary Is...............	Overseas Provinces (Spain)	m13	47
Cape of Good Hope........	Province (S. Africa)	G4	83
Cape Verde Is...........	Overseas Province (Portugal)	o12	79
Caroline Is..............	Districts (Pacific Is., U.S. Trust.)	I16	63
Cayman Is...............	Territory, West Indies Federation	F3	99
Celebes.................	Province (Indonesia)	F6	69
Central African Republic†.....	Republic (Fr. Com.)	G2	81
Central America...........			95
Ceylon†................	Self-gov. Member (Comm. of Nat.)	G7	73
Chad, Republic of †.........	Republic (Fr. Com.)	F7	77
Channel Is..............	Bailiwicks (Br.)	F5	39
Chile†.................	Republic	......	87, 91
China (excl. Formosa).......	People's Republic		65
Colombia†..............	Republic	C3	87
Colorado...............	State (U.S.)	......	115
Comoro Is...............	Possession (Fr.)	C8	83
Congo (Rep. of Congo; Capital: Brazzaville)†......	Republic (Fr. Com.)	G7	77
Congo, The (Rep. of The Congo Capital: Léopoldville)†......	Republic	F8	77
Connecticut.............	State (U.S.)	......	117
Cook Is................	Dependency (N.Z.)	H10	35
Corsica................	Department (France)	C2	49
Costa Rica†.............	Republic	E5	95
Crete..................	Division (Greece)	E5	59
Cuba†.................	Republic	D2	99
Curacao................	Division of Neth. Antilles (Neth.)	B4	87
Cyprus†................	Republic	F6	63
Czechoslovakia†...........	People's Republic	D3	53
Dahomey, Republic of†......	Republic (Fr. Com.)	F6	77
Delaware...............	State (U.S.)	......	135
Denmark†...............	Kingdom	D9	37
District of Columbia.........	District (U.S.)	C1	135
Dominica...............	Territory, West Indies Federation	o16	99
Dominican Republic†........	Republic	F8	99
Easter I................	Part of Valparaiso Prov. (Chile)	*H13	35
Ecuador†...............	Republic	D3	87
Egypt (U.A.R.)...........	Region (United Arab Republic)	D3	81
England & Wales...........	Division of the United Kingdom	......	41
Eritrea................	Autonomous State (Ethiopia)	E5	81

‡ *Census of April 1, 1960 for U.S. states and possessions.*

Region or Political Division	Capital	Population Estimated 1/1/1960‡	Area in sq. miles
Estonia (S.S.R.)	Tallinn	1,235,000	17,410
Ethiopia (incl. Eritrea)†	Addis Ababa	21,351,000	475,800
Europe		573,352,600	3,850,000
Faeroe Is	Thorshavn	36,000	540
Falkland Is. (excl. Deps.)	Port Stanley	2,000	4,618
Fernando Póo	Santa Isabel	44,000	785
Fiji	Suva	385,000	7,055
Finland†	Helsinki	4,435,000	130,085
Florida	Tallahassee	4,951,560	58,560
Formosa (Nationalist China†)	Taipei	10,323,000	13,885
France†	Paris	44,927,000	212,766
French Equatorial Africa		5,015,400	917,931
French Guiana	Cayenne	31,000	35,126
French Oceania	Papeete	144,000	1,544
French Somaliland	Djibouti	69,300	8,492
French West Africa	Dakar	17,696,000	1,694,914
Gabon Republic†	Libreville	434,000	98,283
Galapagos Is	Progreso	1,720	3,042
Gambia	Bathurst	307,000	3,978
Gaza Area	Gaza	365,000	230
Georgia (S.S.R.)	Tbilisi	4,089,000	26,910
Georgia	Atlanta	3,943,116	58,876
Germany (Entire)		72,149,000	137,441
Germany, East	Berlin (East)	16,403,000	41,634
Germany, West (incl. West Berlin)	Bonn	55,746,000	95,819
Ghana†	Accra	4,847,000	91,819
Gibraltar	Gibraltar	26,000	2.3
Gilbert & Ellice Is	Tarawa	41,000	369
Great Britain & Northern Ireland, see United Kingdom			
Greece†	Athens (Athinai)	8,319,000	51,169
Greenland	Godthaab	28,900	839,782
Grenada	St. George's	99,000	133
Guadeloupe (incl. Dependencies)	Basse-Terre	268,000	687
Guam	Agana	42,000	206
Guatemala†	Guatemala	2,584,000	42,031
Guernsey (incl. Dependencies)	St. Peter Port	46,000	30
Guinea, Republic of†	Conakry	2,667,000	94,945
Haiti†	Port-au-Prince	3,492,000	10,711
Hawaii	Honolulu	632,772	6,424
Honduras†	Tegucigalpa	1,915,000	43,266
Hong Kong	Victoria	2,877,000	391
Hungary†	Budapest	9,943,000	35,909

*† Member of the United Nations (1960).   * Not shown on map.*

Region or Political Division	Form of Government and Ruling Power	Index Key	Map Page
Estonia (S.S.R.)	Soviet Socialist Republic (Sov. Un.)	B5	57
Ethiopia (incl. Eritrea)†	Empire	F9	77
Europe			37
Faeroe Is.	Autonomous County (Denmark)	C6	37
Falkland Is. (excl. Deps.)	Colony (Br.)	I4	87
Fernando Póo	Overseas Prov. (Sp.)	F6	77
Fiji	Colony (Br.)	H9	35
Finland†	Republic	F11	55
Florida	State (U.S.)		119
Formosa (Nationalist China†)	Republic	G9	65
France†	Republic (Fr. Union)		43
French Equatorial Africa		*F5	77
French Guiana	Overseas Department (France)	C5	87
French Oceania	Overseas Territory (Fr.)	H11	35
French Somaliland	Overseas Territory (Fr.)	E10	77
French West Africa		*E5	77
Gabon Republic†	Republic, Fr. Com.	G7	77
Galapagos Is.	Province (Ecuador)	C2	87
Gambia	Colony and Protectorate (Br.)	E4	77
Gaza Area	Mil. Occ. (Egypt)	B4	81
Georgia (S.S.R.)	Soviet Socialist Republic (Sov. Un.)	E7	61
Georgia	State (U.S.)		120
Germany (Entire)			45
Germany, East	People's Republic		45
Germany, West (incl. West Berlin)	Federal Republic		45
Ghana†	Republic (Comm. of Nat.)	F5	77
Gibraltar	Colony (Br.)	D3	47
Gilbert & Ellice Is.	Colony (Br.)	G8	35
Great Britain & Northern Ireland, see United Kingdom			
Greece†	Kingdom	C3	59
Greenland	Overseas County (Denmark)	B16	93
Grenada	Territory, West Indies Federation	p16	99
Guadeloupe (incl. Dependencies)	Overseas Department (France)	n15	99
Guam	Unincorporated Territory (U.S.)	F6	35
Guatemala†	Republic	C2	95
Guernsey (incl. Dependencies)	Bailiwick (Br.)	F5	39
Guinea, Republic of†	Republic	E4	77
Haiti†	Republic	F7	99
Hawaii	State (U.S.)		121
Honduras†	Republic	C4	95
Hong Kong	Colony (Br.)	G7	65
Hungary†	People's Republic	B4	51

‡*Census of April 1, 1960 for U.S. states and possessions.*

15

Region or Political Division	Capital	Population Estimated 1/1/1960‡	Area in sq. miles
Iceland†......................	Reykjavik	171,000	39,750
Idaho........................	Boise	667,191	83,557
Ifni.........................	Sidi Ifni	65,000	579
Illinois......................	Springfield	10,081,158	56,400
India† (incl. Kashmir)........	New Delhi	404,333,000	1,269,506
Indiana.....................	Indianapolis	4,662,498	36,291
Indonesia†...................	Djakarta	87,802,000	575,893
Iowa........................	Des Moines	2,757,537	56,290
Iran (Persia)†................	Tehran	20,577,000	629,180
Iraq†........................	Baghdad	6,784,000	171,554
Ireland†.....................	Dublin	2,893,000	27,137
Isle of Man..................	Douglas	57,300	227
Israel†......................	Jerusalem	2,111,000	7,990
Italy†.......................	Rome (Roma)	49,363,000	116,273
Ivory Coast, Republic of†.....	Abidjan	3,145,000	124,550
Jamaica.....................	Kingston	1,702,000	4,411
Japan†......................	Tokyo	93,031,000	142,733
Java and Madoera............	....	55,293,000	51,032
Jersey......................	St. Helier	53,000	45
Jordan†.....................	Amman	1,702,000	37,291
Kansas......................	Topeka	2,178,611	82,264
Kashmir, Jammu &............	Srinagar	4,783,000	82,258
Kazakh [S.S.R.]..............	Alma-Ata	9,478,000	1,064,100
Kentucky....................	Frankfort	3,038,156	40,395
Kenya.......................	Nairobi	6,444,000	224,960
Kirghiz [S.S.R.]..............	Frunze	2,103,000	76,640
Korea (Entire)...............	....	30,917,000	85,239
Korea, North................	Pyongyang	8,083,000	47,811
Korea, South................	Seoul (Soul)	22,834,000	37,414
Kuwait......................	Kuwait	219,000	5,998
Laos†.......................	Vientiane	1,754,000	91,482
Latvia (S.S.R.)...............	Riga	2,134,000	24,600
Lebanon†....................	Beirut	1,719,000	4,014
Leeward Is...................	....	175,300	423
Liberia†.....................	Monrovia	1,350,000	42,989
Libya†......................	Tripoli; Bengasi	1,200,000	679,358
Liechtenstein................	Vaduz	16,000	60.6
Lithuania (S.S.R.)............	Vilnyus	2,757,000	25,170
Louisiana...................	Baton Rouge	3,257,022	48,523
Luxembourg†.................	Luxembourg	320,000	998
Macao......................	Macao	228,000	6.2
Madeira Is...................	Funchal	289,000	308
Maine.......................	Augusta	969,265	33,215
Malagasy (Madagascar).......	Tananarive	5,225,000	228,510
Malaya†.....................	Kuala Lumpur	6,809,000	50,677

† *Member of the United Natins (1960).* * *Not shown on map.*

16

Region or Political Division	Form of Government and Ruling Power	Index Key	Map Page
Iceland†	Republic	n23	55
Idaho	State (U.S.)	.....	123
Ifni	Overseas Prov. (Sp.)	D4	77
Illinois	State (U.S.)	.....	125
India† (incl. Kashmir)	Republic (Commonwealth of Nat.)	.....	73
Indiana	State (U.S.)	.....	127
Indonesia†	Republic	.....	69
Iowa	State (U.S.)	.....	128
Iran (Persia)†	Kingdom	F8	61, 63
Iraq†	Republic	F7	61, 63
Ireland†	Republic	D3	39
Isle of Man	Possession (Br.)	C4	39
Israel†	Republic	F10	59
Italy†	Republic	.....	49
Ivory Coast, Republic of†	Republic (Fr. Com.)	F5	77
Jamaica	Territory, West Indies Federation	F5	95
Japan†	Empire	.....	67
Java and Madoera	Provinces (Indonesia)	G4	69
Jersey	Bailiwick (Br.)	F5	39
Jordan†	Kingdom	G11, F6	59, 61
Kansas	State (U.S.)	.....	129
Kashmir, Jammu &	In dispute (India & Pakistan)	A6	73
Kazakh [S.S.R.]	Soviet Socialist Republic (Sov. Un.)	E8	61
Kentucky	State (U.S.)	.....	130
Kenya	Colony and Protectorate (Br.)	F9	77
Kirghiz [S.S.R.]	Soviet Socialist Republic (Sov. Un.)	E10	61
Korea (Entire)		.....	67
Korea, North	People's Republic	.....	67
Korea, South	Republic	G7	67
Kuwait	Sheikdom (Br. protection)	G7	61, 63
Laos†	Kingdom	B4	71
Latvia (S.S.R.)	Soviet Socialist Republic (Sov. Un.)	C4	57
Lebanon†	Republic	F6	63
Leeward Is.		n15	99
Liberia†	Republic	F4	77
Libya†	Kingdom	D7	77
Liechtenstein	Principality	E4	45
Lithuania (S.S.R.)	Soviet Socialist Republic (Sov. Un.)	D4	57
Louisiana	State (U.S.)	.....	131
Luxembourg†	Grand Duchy	C7	43
Macao	Overseas Province (Portugal)	G7	65
Madeira Is.	Funchal District (Portugal)	C4	77
Maine	State (U.S.)	.....	132
Malagasy (Madagascar)	Republic	I10	77
Malaya†	Protected Federation (Br.)	J4	71

‡ *Census of April 1, 1960 for U.S. states and possessions.*

Region or Political Division	Capital	Population Estimated 1/1/1960‡	Area in sq. miles
Maldive Is.....................	Malé	83,500	115
Mali Republic†...............	Bamako	3,748,000	465,050
Malta.........................	Valletta	325,000	122
Manchuria.....................	....	46,342,000	300,000
Manitoba......................	Winnipeg	894,000	251,030
Mariana Is. (excl. Guam)......	....	10,000	154
Marshall Is...................	Majuro	16,200	70
Martinique....................	Fort-de-France	275,000	425
Maryland......................	Annapolis	3,100,689	10,577
Massachusetts.................	Boston	5,148,578	8,257
Mauritania, Islamic Rep. of†.....	Saint Louis	685,000	419,390
Mauritius (incl. Dependencies)...	Port Louis	650,000	809
Mexico†.......................	Mexico City	33,954,000	758,061
Michigan......................	Lansing	7,823,194	58,216
Midway Island.................		600	2
Minnesota.....................	Saint Paul	3,413,864	84,068
Mississippi...................	Jackson	2,178,141	47,716
Missouri......................	Jefferson City	4,319,813	69,674
Moldavia (S.S.R.).............	Kishinev	2,958,000	13,010
Monaco........................	Monaco	22,500	0.6
Mongolia......................	Ulan Bator	1,056,000	625,950
Montana.......................	Helena	674,767	147,138
Montserrat....................	Plymouth	15,500	32
Morocco†......................	Rabat	10,165,000	170,382
Mozambique....................	Lourenço Marques	6,253,000	297,654
Muscat & Oman.................	Muscat	623,000	81,979
Natal.........................	Pietermaritzburg	2,508,000	33,578
Nauru.........................	....	4,300	8
Nebraska......................	Lincoln	1,411,350	77,227
Nepal†........................	Katmandu	8,978,000	54,362
Netherlands†..................	's Gravenhage (The Hague)	11,389,000	12,526
Netherlands Antilles..........	Willemstad	202,000	371
Netherlands New Guinea.......	Hollandia	754,000	159,375
Nevada........................	Carson City	285,278	110,540
New Brunswick.................	Fredericton	596,000	27,985
New Caledonia (incl. Deps.).....	Nouméa	81,000	7,202
Newfoundland..................	Saint John's	454,000	155,364
New Guinea, Ter. of...........	Port Moresby, Papua	1,409,000	93,000
New Hampshire.................	Concord	606,921	9,304
New Hebrides..................	Vila	60,000	5,700
New Jersey....................	Trenton	6,066,782	7,836
New Mexico....................	Santa Fe	951,023	121,666
New South Wales...............	Sydney	3,758,000	309,433
New York......................	Albany	16,182,304	49,576
New Zealand†..................	Wellington	2,332,000	103,736
Nicaragua†....................	Managua	1,489,000	48,636

† *Member of the United Nations (1960).*   * *Not shown on map.*

Region or Political Division	Form of Government and Ruling Power	Index Key	Map Page
Maldive Is.................	Sultanate (Br. protection)	G5	73
Mali Republic†...........	Republic (Fr. Com.)	E5	77
Malta.....................	Colony (Br.)	H10	37
Manchuria................		B10	65
Manitoba.................	Province (Canada)	......	193
Mariana Is. (excl. Guam)....	Districts (Pacific Is., U.S. Trust.)	E6	35
Marshall Is................	District (Pacific Is., U.S. Trust.)	F7	35
Martinique	Overseas Dept. (Fr.)	o16	99
Maryland..................	State (U.S.)	......	135
Massachusetts............	State (U.S.)	......	137
Mauritania, Islamic Rep. of†...	Republic (Fr. Com.)	D4	77
Mauritius (incl. Dependencies).	Colony (Br.)	*H24	35
Mexico†...................	Federal Republic	......	97
Michigan..................	State (U.S.)	......	139
Midway Island.............	Possession (U.S.)	E9	35
Minnesota.................	State (U.S.)	......	141
Mississippi................	State (U.S.)	......	143
Missouri..................	State (U.S.)	......	145
Moldavia (S.S.R.).........	Soviet Socialist Republic (Sov. Un.)	H7	57
Monaco...................	Principality	F7	43
Mongolia.................	People's Republic	B5	65
Montana..................	State (U.S.)	......	147
Montserrat...............	Territory, West Indies Federation	n15	71
Morocco†.................	Kingdom	C5	77
Mozambique..............	Overseas Province (Portugal)	H9	77
Muscat & Oman...........	Protectorate (Br.)	H8	63
Natal.....................	Province (S. Africa)	I9	77
Nauru....................	Trust Ter., U.N. (Austl., Br., N.Z.)	G8	35
Nebraska.................	State (U.S.)	......	149
Nepal†...................	Kingdom	C7	73
Netherlands†.............	Kingdom	A6, B2	43, 45
Netherlands Antilles........	Overseas Territory (Netherlands)	B4	87
Netherlands New Guinea.....	Provisional (under Neth.)	F9	69
Nevada...................	State (U.S.)	......	151
New Brunswick............	Province (Canada)	......	199
New Caledonia (incl. Deps.)...	Overseas Territory (Fr.)	H7	35
Newfoundland.............	Province (Canada)	......	200
New Guinea, Ter. of........	Trust. Ter., U.N. (Austl.; Papua)	k11	85
New Hampshire............	State (U.S.)	......	153
New Hebrides.............	Condominium (Fr., Br.)	H8	35
New Jersey................	State (U.S.)	......	155
New Mexico...............	State (U.S.)	......	157
New South Wales..........	State (Australia)	F8	85
New York.................	State (U.S.)	......	159
New Zealand†.............	Self-gov. Member (Comm. of Nat.)	I8	35
Nicaragua†................	Republic	D4	95

‡ *Census of April 1, 1960 for U.S. states and possessions.*

19

Region or Political Division	Capital	Population Estimated 1/1/1960‡	Area in sq. miles
Niger, Republic of†	Niamey	2,515,000	459,180
Nigeria, Federation of	Lagos	34,228,000	367,641
Niue	Alofi	5,300	100
Norfolk Island	Kingston	1,150	13
North America		251,054,000	9,435,000
North Borneo	Jesselton	426,000	29,386
North Carolina	Raleigh	4,556,155	52,712
North Dakota	Bismarck	632,446	70,665
Northern Ireland	Belfast	1,425,000	5,439
Northern Rhodesia	Lusaka	2,377,000	288,129
Northern Territory	Darwin	38,000	523,620
Northwest Territories	Ottawa, Ontario	22,000	1,304,903
Norway†	Oslo	3,574,000	125,032
Nova Scotia	Halifax	719,000	21,068
Nyasaland	Zomba	2,788,000	49,177
Oceania		16,054,000	3,552,000
Ohio	Columbus	9,706,397	41,222
Oklahoma	Oklahoma City	2,328,284	69,919
Ontario	Toronto	6,040,000	412,582
Orange Free State	Bloemfontein	1,089,000	49,866
Oregon	Salem	1,768,687	96,981
Pacific Island Trust Ter.	Agana, Guam	77,000	685
Pakistan† (excl. Kashmir)	Rawalpindi	86,733,000	364,702
Pakistan, East	Dacca	44,178,000	54,501
Pakistan, West (incl. Karachi)		42,555,000	310,201
Palau (Pelew) Is.		8,700	188
Panama†	Panamá	1,040,000	28,745
Papua (excl. New Guinea Ter.)	Port Moresby	516,000	90,540
Paraguay†	Asunción	1,736,000	157,006
Pennsylvania	Harrisburg	11,319,366	45,333
Peru†	Lima	10,640,000	482,133
Philippines†	Quezon City	23,721,000	115,600
Pitcairn (excl. Dependencies)	Adamstown	150	2
Poland†	Warsaw (Warszawa)	29,550,000	120,327
Portugal†	Lisbon (Lisboa)	9,108,000	35,589
Portuguese Guinea	Bissau	563,000	13,948
Port. India (Goa, Damão, Diu)	Nova Goa	647,000	1,618
Portuguese Timor	Dili	491,000	7,332
Prince Edward Island	Charlottetown	103,000	2,184
Puerto Rico	San Juan	2,403,000	3,435
Qatar	Doha	41,800	8,497
Quebec	Quebec	5,070,000	594,860
Queensland	Brisbane	1,446,000	670,600

*† Member of the United Nations (1960). * Not shown on map.*

Region or Political Division	Form of Government and Ruling Power	Index Key	Map Page
Niger, Republic of†	Republic (Fr. Com.)	E6	77
Nigeria, Federation of	Self-gov. Member (Comm. of Nat.)	F6	77
Niue	Dependency (N.Z.)	*H9	35
Norfolk Island	External Territory (Australia)	*H7	35
North America			93
North Borneo	Colony (Br.)	D5	69
North Carolina	State (U.S.)		163
North Dakota	State (U.S.)		165
Northern Ireland	Division of the United Kingdom	C3	39
Northern Rhodesia	Protectorate (Rhodesia & Nya., Br.)	H8	77
Northern Territory	Territory (Australia)	C5	85
Northwest Territories	Territory (Canada)		101
Norway†	Kingdom	G3	55
Nova Scotia	Province (Canada)	E4	199
Nyasaland	Protectorate (Rh.&Nya.,Fed.of,Br.)	H9	77
Oceania			35
Ohio	State (U.S.)		167
Oklahoma	State (U.S.)		169
Ontario	Province (Canada)		195
Orange Free State	Province (S. Africa)	I8	77
Oregon	State (U.S.)		171
Pacific Island Trust Ter.	Trust Territory, U.N. (U.S.)	F7	35
Pakistan† (excl. Kashmir)	Republic (Commonwealth of Nat.)	C4, D9	73
Pakistan, East	East Bengal Province (Pakistan)	D9	73
Pakistan, West (incl. Karachi)	Provinces (Pakistan)	C4	73
Palau (Pelew) Is.	Part of Pacific Is. (U.S. Trust.)	I16	69
Panama†	Republic	F7	95
Papua (excl. New Guinea Ter.)	External Territory (Australia)	k11	85
Paraguay†	Republic	F5, C1	87, 89
Pennsylvania	State (U.S.)		173
Peru†	Republic	D3	87
Philippines†	Republic	B6	69
Pitcairn (excl. Dependencies)	Colony (Br.)	H12	34
Poland†	People's Republic	C5	53
Portugal†	Republic	C1	47
Portuguese Guinea	Overseas Province (Portugal)	F1	79
Port. India (Goa, Damão, Diu)	Overseas Provinces (Portugal)	E5	73
Portuguese Timor	Overseas Province (Portugal)	G7	69
Prince Edward Island	Province (Canada)	C6	199
Puerto Rico	Commonwealth (U.S.)	m13	99
Qatar	Sheikdom (Br. protection)	C8	81
Quebec	Province (Canada)		97
Queensland	State (Australia)	D7	85

‡ *Census of April 1, 1960 for U.S. states and possessions.*

Region or Political Division	Capital	Population Estimated 1/1/1960‡	Area in sq. miles
Reunion	St. Denis	334,000	923.7
Rhode Island	Providence	859,488	1,214
Rhodesia & Nyasaland, Federation of	Salisbury	7,805,000	487,639
Rio Muni		169,670	10,043
Romania†	Bucharest (Bucuresti)	18,398,000	91,675
Ruanda-Urundi	Usumbura	4,941,000	20,916
Russian Soviet Federated Socialist Republic (incl. Karelia)	Moscow (Moskva)	119,811,000	6,593,390
Ryukyu Is. (Southern).°°°	Naha	862,000	881
Saar	Saarbrücken	1,036,000	991
Saharan Departments		645,000	838,414
St. Helena (incl. Dependencies)	Jamestown	5,900	119
St. Kitts-Nevis-Anguilla	Basseterre	62,000	153
St. Lucia	Castries	96,000	233
St. Pierre & Miquelon	St. Pierre	5,100	92.6
St. Vincent	Kingstown	86,000	150
Salvador, El†	San Salvador	2,556,000	8,260
Samoa, American°	Pago Pago	23,000	76
Samoa, Western	Apia	106,000	1,133
San Marino	San Marino	15,100	23
Sao Tome & Principe	São Tomé	65,000	372
Sarawak	Kuching	670,000	47,069
Sardinia	Cagliari	1,456,000	9,301
Saskatchewan	Regina	906,000	251,700
Saudi Arabia†	Riyadh and Mecca	6,159,000	617,600
Scotland	Edinburgh	5,225,000	30,409
Senegal, Republic of†	Saint Louis	2,337,000	76,153
Seychelles	Victoria	47,500	156
Sicily	Palermo	4,656,000	9,925
Sierra Leone	Freetown	2,185,000	27,924
Sikkim	Gangtok	152,000	2,745
Singapore (incl. Deps.)	Singapore	1,595,000	289
Solomon Is. (Austl. Trust.)	Sohano	58,000	4,100
Solomon Is., British	Honiara	106,500	11,500
Somalia	Mogadiscio	2,047,000	246,137
South Africa†	Pretoria and Cape Town	14,435,000	472,733
South America.°°		137,346,500	6,860,000
South Australia	Adelaide	915,000	380,070
South Carolina	Columbia	2,382,594	31,055
South Dakota	Pierre	680,514	77,047
Southern Rhodesia	Salisbury	2,640,000	150,327
South-West Africa	Windhoek	608,000	317,725
Soviet Union (Union of Soviet Socialist Republics)†	Moscow (Moskva)	212,801,000	8,650,140

† *Member of the United Nations (1960).* *Not shown on map.*

Region or Political Division	Form of Government and Ruling Power	Index Key	Map Page
Reunion	Overseas Department (France)	H24	35
Rhode Island	State (U.S.)	......	117
Rhodesia & Nyasaland, Federation of	Semi-Auton Dependencies (Br.)	H8	77
Rio Muni	Overseas Prov. (Sp.)	H6	79
Romania†	People's Republic	B7	51
Ruanda-Urundi	Kingdoms	I3	81
Russian Soviet Federated Socialist Republic (incl. Karelia)	Soviet Federated Socialist Republic (Sov. Un.)	C11	61
Ryukyu Is. (Southern)	Military Government (U.S.)	F10	65
Saar	State (West Germany)	D3	45
Saharan Departments	Overseas Depts. (Fr.)	C4	75
St. Helena (incl. Dependencies)	Colony (Br.)	H5	77
St. Kitts-Nevis-Anguilla	Territory, West Indies Federation	n15	99
St. Lucia	Territory, West Indies Federation	p16	99
St. Pierre & Miquelon	Overseas Territory (Fr.)	D7	200
St. Vincent	Territory, West Indies Federation	p16	99
Salvador, El†	Republic	D3	95
Samoa, American	Unincorporated Territory (U.S.)	G9	35
Samoa, Western	Trust Territory, U.N. (N.Z.)	G9	35
San Marino	Republic	C4	49
Sao Tome & Principe	Overseas Provinces (Portugal)	F6	77
Sarawak	Colony (Br.)	E4	69
Sardinia	Provinces (Italy)	D2	49
Saskatchewan	Province (Canada)	......	193
Saudi Arabia†	Kingdom	G7	63
Scotland	Kingdom (Gt. Br. & N. Ire.)	B4	39
Senegal, Republic of†	Republic (Fr. Com.)	E4	77
Seychelles	Colony (Br.)	G24	35
Sicily	Autonomous Region (Italy)	F4	49
Sierra Leone	Self-gov. Member (Comm. of Nat.)	F4	77
Sikkim	Protectorate (India)	D12	75
Singapore (incl. Deps.)	Self-gov. State (Br.-Comm. of Nat.)	L5	71
Solomon Is. (Austl. Trust.)	New Guinea Ter. (Austl. Trust.)	G7	35
Solomon Is., British	Protectorate (Br.)	G7	35
Somalia	Republic	F10	77
South Africa†	Republic	J7	77
South America			87
South Australia	State (Australia)	E5	85
South Carolina	State (U.S.)	......	174
South Dakota	State (U.S.) ¶	......	165
Southern Rhodesia	Colony (Rh. & Nya., Fed. of, Br.)	I8	77
South-West Africa	Mandate (S. Africa)	I7	77
Soviet Union (Union of Soviet Socialist Republics)†	Federal Soviet Republic	......	61

‡*Census of April 1, 1960 for U.S. states and possessions.*

23

Region or Political Division	Capital	Population Estimated 1/1/1960‡	Area in sq. miles
Spain†	Madrid	30,090,000	194,945
Spanish Guinea	Santa Isabel	216,000	10,830
Spanish Sahara		13,000	102,672
Spanish West Africa		78,000	115,780
Sudan†	Khartoum	11,549,000	967,248
Sumatra		13,848,000	164,198
Surinam (Neth. Guiana)	Paramaribo	254,000	55,144
Svalbard (Spitsbergen)	Longyearbyen	1,100	23,979
Swaziland	Mbabane	277,000	6,705
Sweden†	Stockholm	7,468,000	173,577
Switzerland	Bern	5,246,000	15,944
Syria (U.A.R.)	Damascus	4,556,000	71,209
Tadzhik [S.S.R.]	Stalinabad	2,013,000	55,200
Tanganyika	Dar es Salaam	9,052,000	362,674
Tasmania	Hobart	344,000	26,215
Tennessee	Nashville	3,567,089	42,244
Texas	Austin	9,579,677	267,339
Thailand (Siam)†	Bangkok (Krung Thep)	22,003,000	198,404
Tibet	Lhasa	1,699,000	469,194
Tobago	Scarborough	37,000	116
Togo, Republic of†	Lomé	1,136,000	22,002
Tokelau (Union Is.)		2,000	4
Tonja	Nukualofa	62,000	269
Transvaal	Pretoria	5,337,000	110,450
Trinidad	Port-of-Spain	785,500	1,979
Tristan da Cunha	Edinburgh	330	45
Trucial Coast		91,000	32,269
Tunisia†	Tunis	3,987,000	48,319
Turkey†	Ankara	26,494,000	299,992
Turkmen [S.S.R.]	Ashkhabad	1,554,000	188,420
Uganda	Entebbe	5,892,000	93,981
Ukraine (S.S.R.)†	Kiyev	42,803,000	232,050
United Arab Republic†	Cairo	29,869,000	457,309
United Kingdom of Great Britain & Northern Ireland†	London	58,591,000	94,194
United States†	Washington	179,323,175	3,675,633
Upper Volta, Republic of†	Ouagadougou	3,516,000	105,879
Uruguay†	Montevideo	2,709,000	72,172
Utah	Salt Lake City	890,627	84,916
Uzbek [S.S.R.]	Tashkent	8,187,000	158,070
Vatican City		1,050	0.2
Venezuela†	Caracas	6,622,000	352,051
Vermont	Montpelier	389,881	9,609
Victoria	Melbourne	2,790,000	87,884
Vietnam (Entire)		27,776,000	127,250

† *Member of the United Nations (1960).* * *Not shown on map.*

24

Region or Political Division	Form of Government and Ruling Power	Index Key	Map Page
Spain†	Kingdom (Regency)	......	47
Spanish Guinea		F6	77
Spanish Sahara	Overseas Provinces (Sp.)	D4	77
Spanish West Africa	Governorate (Spain)	D4	77
Sudan†	Republic	E8	77
Sumatra	Provinces (Indonesia)	E1	69
Surinam (Neth. Guiana)	Overseas Territory (Netherlands)	C5	87
Svalbard (Spitsbergen)	Dependency (Norway)	B5	61
Swaziland	Prot. Territory (Br.)	I9	77
Sweden†	Kingdom	H5	55
Switzerland	Federal Republic	E3	45
Syria (U.A.R.)	Region (United Arab Republic)	F6	63
Tadzhik [S.S.R.]	Soviet Socialist Republic (Sov. Un.)	F10	61
Tanganyika	Trust Territory, U.N. (Br.)	G9	77
Tasmania	State (Australia)	o15	85
Tennessee	State (U.S.)	......	175
Texas	State (U.S.)	......	177,179
Thailand (Siam)†	Kingdom	E4	71
Tibet	Autonomous Region (China)	F11	63
Tobago	Territory, West Indies Federation	B4	87
Togo, Republic of†	Republic (Fr. protection)	F6	77
Tokelau (Union Is.)	Dependency (N.Z.)	G9	35
Tonja	Protected Kingdom (Br.)	H9	35
Transvaal	Province (S. Africa)	E5	83
Trinidad	Territory, West Indies Federation	B4	87
Tristan da Cunha	Dependency (St. Helena, Br.)	I20	35
Trucial Coast	Sheikdoms	G8	63
Tunisia†	Republic	C6	77
Turkey†	Republic	F6	63
Turkmen [S.S.R.]	Soviet Socialist Republic (Sov. Un.)	F8	61
Uganda	Protectorate (Br.)	F9	77
Ukraine (S.S.R.)†	Soviet Socialist Republic (Sov. Un.)	G6	57
United Arab Republic†	Republic	D8, C9	77
United Kingdom of Great Britain & Northern Ireland	Kingdom	......	39
United States†	Federal Republic	......	103
Upper Volta, Republic of†	Republic (Fr. Com.)	E5	77
Uruguay†	Republic	G5	87
Utah	State (U.S.)	......	181
Uzbek [S.S.R.]	Soviet Socialist Republic (Sov. Un.)	E9	61
Vatican City	Ecclesiastical State	D4	49
Venezuela†	Federal Republic	C4	87
Vermont	State (U.S.)	......	153
Victoria	State (Australia)	G7	85
Vietnam (Entire)		D8	71

‡*Census of April 1, 1960 for U.S. states and possessions.*

Region or Political Division	Capital	Population [Estimated 1/1/1960‡	Area in sq. miles
Vietnam, North...............	Hanoi	14,788,000	61,516
Vietnam, South...............	Saigon	12,988,000	65,709
Virgin Is. (British)...........	Road Town	8,300	67
Virgin Is. (of the U.S.).........	Charlotte Amalie	32,000	133
Virginia......................	Richmond	3,966,949	40,815
Wales (incl. Monmouthshire)....	Cardiff	2,991,000	8,016
Washington..................	Olympia	2,853,214	68,192
Western Australia.............	Perth	722,000	975,920
West Indies, The (Federation)....	Port-of-Spain	3,279,000	8,005
West Virginia.................	Charleston	1,860,421	24,181
White Russia (S.S.R.)†..........	Minsk	8,140,000	80,150
Windward Is..................		550,300	820
Wisconsin....................	Madison	3,951,777	56,154
World.......................		2,930,050,000	57,467,000
Wyoming....................	Cheyenne	330,006	97,914
Yemen†.:::...................	San'a	4,900,000	75,270
Yugoslavia†.::...............	Belgrade (Beograd)	18,796,000	98,742
Yukon......................	Whitehorse	14,000	207,076
Zanzibar::::.................	Zanzibar	178,000	1,020

*† Member of the United Nations (1960).   * Not shown on map.*

INDEX OF THE WORLD—*Continued*

Region or Political Division	Form of Government and Ruling Power	Index Key	Map Page
Vietnam, North	People's Republic	C7	71
Vietnam, South	Republic	F8	71
Virgin Is. (British)	Colony (Leeward Is., Br.)	m14	99
Virgin Is. (of the U.S.)	Unincorporated Territory (U.S.)	m14	99
Virginia	State (U.S.)	......	183
Wales (incl. Monmouthshire)	Counties (Eng. & Wales, Gt. Br.)	B4	41
Washington	State (U.S.)	......	185
Western Australia	State (Australia)	......	85
West Indies, The (Federation)	Self-gov. Dominion (Comm. of Nat.)	......	99
West Virginia	State (U.S.)	......	183
White Russia (S.S.R.)†	Soviet Socialist Republic (Sov. Un.	E7	57
Windward Is.	......	n15	99
Wisconsin	State (U.S.)	......	187
World	......	......	35
Wyoming	State (U.S.)	......	189
Yemen†	Kingdom	E10	77
Yugoslavia†	Federal People's Republic	......	51
Yukon	Territory (Canada)	D5	101
Zanzibar	Protected Sultanate (Br.)	G10	77

‡*Census of April 1, 1960 for U.S. states and possessions.*

WORLD FACTS AND COMPARISONS

MOVEMENTS OF THE EARTH

The earth makes one complete revolution around the sun every 365 days, 5 hours, 48 minutes, and 46 seconds.

The earth makes one complete rotation on its axis in 23 hours and 56 minutes.

The earth revolves in its orbit around the sun at a speed of 66,700 miles per hour.

The earth rotates on its axis at an equatorial speed of more than 1,000 miles per hour.

MEASUREMENTS OF THE EARTH

Estimated age of the earth, at least 3 billion years.

Equatorial diameter of the earth, 7,926.68 miles.

Polar diameter of the earth, 7,899.99 miles.

Mean diameter of the earth, 7,918.78 miles.

Equatorial circumference of the earth, 24,902.45 miles.

Polar circumference of the earth, 24,818.60 miles.

Difference between equatorial and polar circumference of the earth, 83.85 miles.

Weight of the earth, 6,600,000,000,000,000,000,000,000 tons, or 6,600 billion billion tons.

Total area of the earth, 196,940,400 square miles.

Total land area of the earth (including inland water but excluding Antarctica), 52,125,000 square miles.

THE EARTH'S INHABITANTS

Total population of the earth is estimated to be 2,930,050,000 (January 1, 1960).

Estimated population density of the earth, 56 per square mile.

THE EARTH'S SURFACE

Highest point on the earth's surface, Mount Everest, China (Tibet)–Nepal, 29,028 feet.

Lowest point on the earth's land surface, shores of the Dead Sea, Palestine, 1,286 feet below sea level.

Greatest ocean depth, the Challenger Deep, south of Guam, Pacific Ocean, 35,800 feet.

EXTREMES OF TEMPERATURE AND RAINFALL OF THE EARTH

Highest temperature ever recorded, 136°F. at Azizia, Libya, Africa, on September 13, 1922.

Lowest temperature ever recorded, −125.3°F. at Vostok, Antarctica, on August 25, 1958.

Highest mean annual temperature, 86°F. at Massaua, Ethiopia, and at Djibouti, French Somaliland, Africa.

Lowest mean annual temperature, −22°F. at Eismitte, Greenland (70° 54′ N. Lat., 40° 42′ W. Long.).

At Baguio, Luzon, in the Philippines, 46 inches of rainfall was reported in a 24-hour period, July 14–15, 1911. This is believed to be the world's record for a 24-hour rainfall.

An authenticated rainfall of 366 inches in 1 month—July, 1861—was reported at Cherrapunji, India. More than 150 inches fell in a period of 5 consecutive days in August, 1841. Average annual rainfall at Cherrapunji is 426 inches.

CONTINENTAL COMPARISONS

CONTINENT	Area (sq. mi.)	Population Estimated Jan. 1, 1960	Population per sq. mi.	Mean Elevation (feet)	Highest Elevation (feet)	Lowest Elevation (feet)
Africa.........	11,635,000	233,719,000	20	1,900	Mt. Kilimanjaro, Tanganyika, 19,590	Qattara Depression, Egypt, 436 below sea level
Antarctica.........	5,100,000	Uninhabited	...	6,000	Mt. Fridtjof Nansen, 18,953	Sea level
Asia.........	17,035,000	1,691,328,000	99	3,000	Mt. Everest, China (Tibet)–Nepal, 29,028	Dead Sea, Palestine, 1,286 below sea level
Australia.........	2,974,581	10,050,000	3	1,000	Mt. Kosciusko, 7,328	Lake Eyre, 39 below sea level
Europe.........	3,850,000	573,353,000	149	980	Mt. Elbrus, Soviet Union, 18,468	Caspian Sea, Soviet Union, 92 below sea level
North America......	9,435,000	251,054,000	27	2,000	Mt. McKinley, United States (Alaska), 20,320	Death Valley, California, 282 below sea level
South America......	6,860,000	137,347,000	20	1,800	Mt. Aconcagua, Argentina, 22,834	Valdes Depression, Argentina, 131 below sea level

PRINCIPAL WORLD CITIES

Addis Ababa, Ethiopia........129,000
Adelaide, Australia (*529,000)...75,100
Ahmadabad, India (*793,813)..788,333
Alexandria (El Iskandarîya),
  Egypt, U.A.R...........1,105,000
Algiers (Alger), Algeria
  (*587,570)............361,285
Amsterdam, Netherlands
  (*1,150,000)..........858,702
Antwerpen (Antwerp), Belgium
  (*895,000)............256,126
Athens (Athinai), Greece
  (*1,378,586)..........565,084
Atlanta, Georgia (*1,011,100)..487,455
Auckland, New Zealand
  (*381,000)............136,540
Baghdad, Iraq............730,549
Baku, Soviet Union
  (*1,060,000)..........968,000
Baltimore, Maryland
  (*1,636,500)..........939,024
Bangalore, India...........778,977
Bangkok (Kung Thep),
  Thailand............830,000
Barcelona, Spain
  (*1,690,000)..........1,428,777
Belfast, Northern Ireland......450,800
Belgrade (Beograd),
  Yugoslavia............470,172
Berlin, East, Germany.....1,200,000
Berlin, West, Germany
  (*3,900,000)..........2,200,000
Birmingham, England
  (*2,525,000)..........1,110,800
Bogotá, Colombia (*715,000)..638,562
Bombay, India...........3,211,000
Boston, Massachusetts
  (*2,913,500)..........697,197
Brussels (Bruxelles), Belgium
  (*1,360,000)..........171,020
Bucharest (Bucureşti),
  Romania (*1,250,000).....1,177,661
Budapest, Hungary.........1,850,000
Buenos Aires, Argentina...
  (*5,850,000)..........3,673,575
Buffalo, New York
  (*1,330,000)..........532,759
Cairo (Al Qāhirah), Egypt,
  U.A.R..............2,447,000
Calcutta, India (*3,750,000)..2,548,677
Canton, China...........1,820,523
Cape Town, South Africa
  (*709,200)............528,700
Caracas, Venzuela
  (*1,425,000)..........700,000
Casablanca, Morocco........682,388
Changchun (Hsinking), China.975,000
Chelyabinsk, Soviet Union
  (*860,000)............688,000
Chengtu, China...........1,107,000
Chicago Illinois (*6,517,600).3,550,404
Chungking (Chungching),
  China..............1,700,000
Cincinnati, Ohio (*1,203,300)..502,550
Cleveland, Ohio (*2,090,800)...876,050
Colombo, Ceylon (*725,000)...423,481
Copenhagen (Köbenhavn),
  Denmark (*1,189,177).......760,820
Dacca, Pakistan (*411,279)...276,033

Dairen (Talien), China........766,400
Dallas, Texas (*1,022,300).....679,684
Damascus (Esh Sham),
  Syria, U.A.R...........408,774
Delhi, India (*1,039,013).....914,790
Denver, Colorado (*858,300)...493,887
Detroit, Michigan
  (*4,028,500)..........1,670,144
Djakarta (Batavia), Indonesia
  (*1,871,200)..........1,492,100
Dublin (Baile Atha Cliath),
  Ireland (*649,338).........539,476
Düsseldorf, Germany (West)
  (*965,000)............594,800
Edinburgh, Scotland.........466,900
Essen, Germany (West)
  (*4,665,000)..........660,000
Frankfurt [am Main], Germany
  (West) (*910,000).........601,700
Fushun, China............678,000
Genève (Geneva), Switzerland
  (*178,900)............155,300
Genova (Genoa), Italy.......711,500
Glasgow, Scotland
  (*1,600,000)..........1,081,700
Gorkiy (Gorki), Soviet Union
  (*1,250,000)..........942,000
Guadalajara, Mexico.........377,928
Hamburg, Germany (West).1,646,600
Harbin, China............1,552,000
Havana (Habana), Cuba
  (*1,217,674)..........785,455
Helsinki, Finland (*456,474)..359,813
Hiroshima, Japan..........357,287
Houston, Texas (*1,251,700)..938,219
Hsian (Sian), China........750,000
Hyderabad, India.........1,085,722
Ibadan, Nigeria...........459,199
Indianapolis, Indiana
  (*806,900)............476,258
Istanbul, Turkey.........1,000,022
Jerusalem, Israel (*219,600)...146,000
Jerusalem, Jordan..........46,713
Johannesburg, South Africa
  (*1,775,000)..........745,000
Kanpur (Cawnpore), India
  (*705,383)............636,443
Kansas City, Missouri
  (*1,025,900)..........475,539
Karachi, Pakistan
  (*1,009,438)..........905,781
Katowice (Stalinogrod), Poland
  (*1,600,000)..........198,000
Kharkov, Soviet Union.......930,000
Kingston, Jamaica (*289,245)..137,700
Kiyev (Kiev), Soviet Union...820,000
Kobe, Japan............979,305
Köln (Cologne), Germany
  (West) (*1,340,000).......670,300
Kowloon, Hong Kong.......1,050,000
Kuala Lumpur, Malaya......315,040
Kunming, China..........880,000
Kuybyshev, Soviet Union....806,000
Kyoto, Japan...........1,204,084
Lahore, Pakistan (*849,476)..789,400
La Paz, Bolivia...........321,073
Leeds, England (*950,000).....508,600
Leipzig, Germany (East)
  (*775,000)............607,655

*Population of metropolitan area, including suburbs.

30

AND POPULATIONS

Leningrad, Soviet Union
(*3,840,000). 3,300,000
Léopoldville, The Congo. 283,900
Lille, France (*760,000). 194,616
Lima, Peru (*950,000). 767,054
Lisbon (Lisboa), Portugal
(*1,100,000). 783,226
Liverpool, England
(*1,470,000). 773,700
London, England
(*10,450,000). 3,273,000
Los Angeles, California
(*6,565,000). 2,479,015
Lyon, France (*755,000). 471,270
Madras, India. 1,596,000
Madrid, Spain. 1,848,901
Manchester, England
(*1,990,000). 686,000
Manila, Philippines
(*1,510,000). 983,906
Mannheim, Germany (West)
(*500,000). 272,300
Marseille, France (*725,000). . .661,492
Melbourne, Australia
(*1,677,100). 128,820
Mexico City, Mexico
(*3,015,000). 2,233,941
Miami, Florida (*1,212,000). . .291,688
Milano (Milan), Italy
(*1,640,000). 1,305,400
Milwaukee, Wisconsin
(*1,240,700). 741,324
Minneapolis, Minnesota
(*1,441,700). 482,872
Minsk, Soviet Union. 509,000
Montevideo, Uruguay. 845,000
Montreal, Canada
(*1,595,000). 1,109,439
Moscow (Moskva), Soviet Union
(*7,000,000). 4,839,000
Mukden (Shenyang), China. .2,411,000
München (Munich), Germany
(West) (*1,275,000). 906,500
Nagoya, Japan. 1,336,780
Nanking, China. 1,419,000
Napoli (Naples), Italy
(*1,275,000). 1,059,100
Nashville, Tennessee
(*411,500). 170,874
Newcastle-on-Tyne, England
(*835,332). 277,100
New Delhi, India. 276,314
New Orleans, Louisiana
(*885,200). 627,525
New York, New York
(*15,404,300). 7,781,984
Novosibirsk, Soviet Union. . . .887,000
Osaka, Japan (*5,300,000). . .2,547,319
Oslo, Norway (*520,000). 437,184
Ottawa, Canada (*345,460). . . .222,129
Paris, France (*6,650,000). . .2,850,189
Peking (Peiping), China. 4,010,000
Philadelphia, Pennsylvania
(*3,969,500). 2,002,512
Phnom Penh, Cambodia. 123,883
Pittsburgh, Pennsylvania
(*1,957,700). 604,332
Prague (Praha),
Czechoslovakia. 922,284

Pretoria, South Africa
(*335,300). 265,900
Pusan, Korea (South). 1,049,363
Pyongyang, Korea (North). . . .450,000
Rangoon, Burma. 752,000
Rio de Janeiro, Brazil
(*3,380,000). 2,940,045
Rome (Roma), Italy. 1,750,700
Rostov [-na-Donu], Soviet
Union. 597,000
Rotterdam, Netherlands
(*915,000). 704,646
Saigon, Vietnam (South). . . .1,614,200
St. Louis, Missouri
(*2,050,800). 750,026
San Diego, California
(*1,065,000). 573,224
San Francisco, California
(*3,275,000). 742,855
San Juan, Puerto Rico
(*465,745). 357,205
Santiago, Chile (*2,075,000). .794,900
São Paulo, Brazil. 3,417,208
Seattle, Washington
(*938,400). 557,087
Seoul (Keijo), Korea (South). 1,574,868
Shanghai, China. 6,900,000
Sheffield, England (*660,000). .499,000
Singapore, Singapore
(*1,675,000). 679,659
Sofia (Sofiya), Bulgaria
(*725,756). 612,270
Stalino, Soviet Union
(*1,050,000). 701,000
Stockholm Sweden
(*1,042,154). 785,945
Stuttgart, Germany (West)
(*750,000). 566,000
Surabaja (Soerabaja),
Indonesia. 935,700
Sverdlovsk, Soviet Union
(*845,000). 777,000
Sydney, Australia
(*1,975,020). 230,330
Taipei (Taihoku), Formosa. . . .503,086
Taiyüan, China. 252,000
Tashkent, Soviet Union. 911,000
Tehrān, Iran (*1,590,000). . .1,513,164
Tel Aviv [-Jaffa], Israel
(*501,800). 363,500
The Hague ('s Gravenhage),
Netherlands (*690,000). 590,755
Tientsin, China. 3,220,000
Tōkyō, Japan (*10,350,000). .6,969,104
Torino (Turin), Italy
(*910,000). 783,100
Toronto, Canada (*1,450,000). .667,706
Tsingtao (Chingtao), China. .1,121,000
Tunis, Tunisia. 410,000
Venezia (Venice), Italy. 327,700
Victoria, Hong Kong
(*2,150,000). 1,000,000
Vienna (Wein), Austria
(*1,900,000). 1,616,125
Warsaw (Warszawa), Poland. . .996,000
Washington, D.C. (*2,053,600). 763,956
Yawata, Japan (*1,100,000). . .286,241
Yokohama, Japan. 1,143,687
Zürich, Switzerland (*438,300). 409,300

31

LARGEST METROPOLITAN AREAS AND CITIES, 1961

Rank 1961		Estimated Population, 1/1/1961	
		Metropolitan Area	City Proper
1	New York	15,550,000	7,775,000
2	Tokyo–Yokohama*	14,200,000	8,360,000
3	London	10,825,000	3,190,000
4	Moscow (Moskva)	8,150,000	6,150,000
5	Osaka–Kobe*	8,075,000	3,030,000
6	Shanghai**	7,600,000	10,400,000
7	Paris	7,600,000	3,025,000
8	Los Angeles	6,725,000	2,510,000
9	Chicago	6,590,000	3,545,000
10	Buenos Aires	6,500,000	2,825,000
11	Calcutta	6,425,000	2,825,000
12	Mexico City	4,900,000	2,725,000
13	Essen–Dortmund–Duisburg*	4,775,000	727,000
14	São Paulo	4,600,000	3,900,000
15	Bombay	4,300,000	3,850,000
16	Rio de Janeiro	4,250,000	3,150,000
17	Detroit–Windsor*	4,070,000	1,655,000
18	Philadelphia	4,005,000	1,995,000
19	Berlin (East and West)	4,000,000	3,240,000
20	Peking**	3,800,000	6,650,000

Rank 1961		Estimated Population, 1/1/1961	
		Metropolitan Area	City Proper
21	Leningrad	3,800,000	3,125,000
22	Cairo	3,750,000	3,225,000
23	San Francisco–Oakland–San José*	3,340,000	740,000
24	Tientsin**	3,100,000	3,500,000
25	Boston	2,930,000	690,000
26	Hong Kong (Victoria)	2,650,000	1,125,000
27	Manila	2,575,000	1,155,000
28	Birmingham (England)	2,540,000	1,093,000
29	Mukden (Shenyang)	2,500,000	2,500,000
30	Wuhan	2,400,000	2,400,000
31	Milano (Milan)	2,375,000	1,475,000
32	Hamburg	2,250,000	1,835,000
33	Djakarta	2,200,000	1,750,000
34	Madras	2,175,000	1,900,000
35	Rome (Roma)	2,175,000	2,025,000
36	Sydney	2,165,000	180,000
37	Delhi–New Delhi*	2,150,000	975,000
38	Budapest	2,140,000	1,825,000
39	Cleveland	2,115,000	875,000
40	Washington	2,100,000	759,000

* City proper population is for first-named city only. ** Municipal boundaries of Shanghai, Peking, and Tientsin now include extensive rural zones, which have been excluded in estimating their metropolitan populations.

POLAR MAP OF THE WORLD

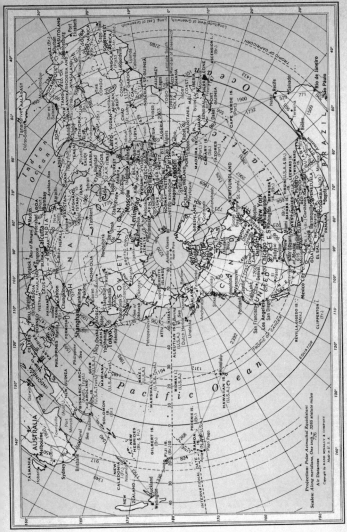

Projection: Polar Azimuthal Equidistant
Scales. Along meridians, One inch = 3265 statute miles
Air Distances
Copyright by RAND McNALLY & COMPANY
Made in U. S. A.

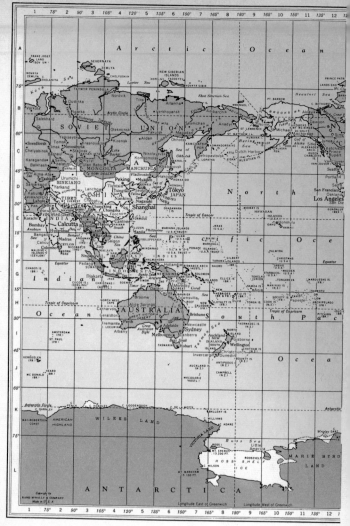

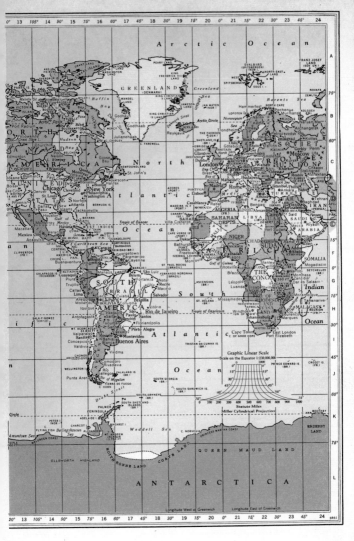

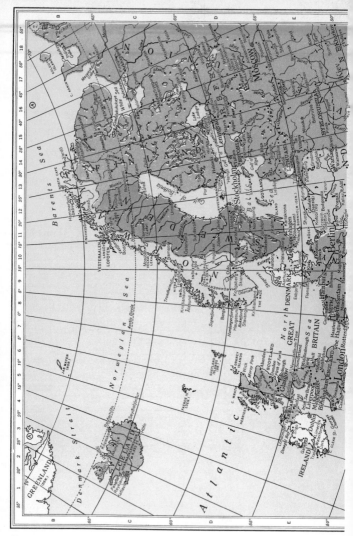

Conic Projection
SCALE 1 : 27,680,000   1 Inch = 436 Statute Miles

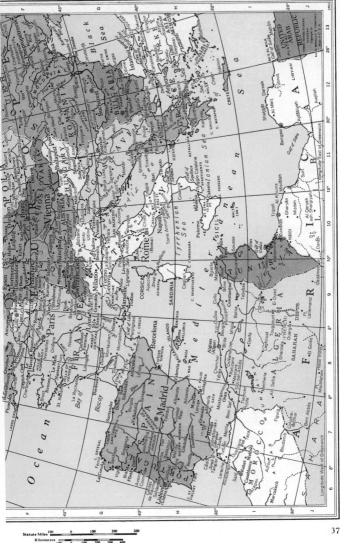

Statute Miles 100 0 100 200 300
Kilometers 100 0 100 200 300 400

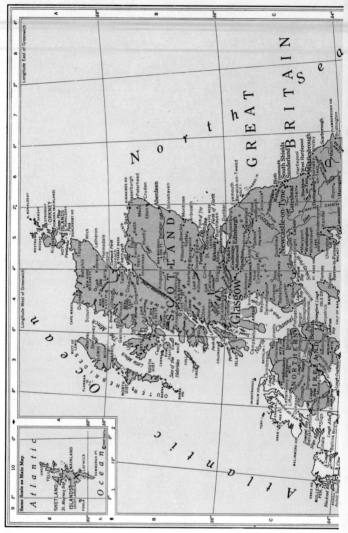

Conic Projection
SCALE 1 : 6,920,000   1 Inch = 109 Statute Miles

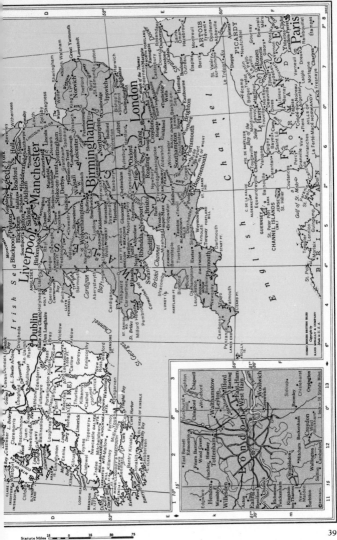

Lambert Conformal Conic Projection
SCALE 1 : 3,460,000   1 Inch = 55.5 Statute Miles

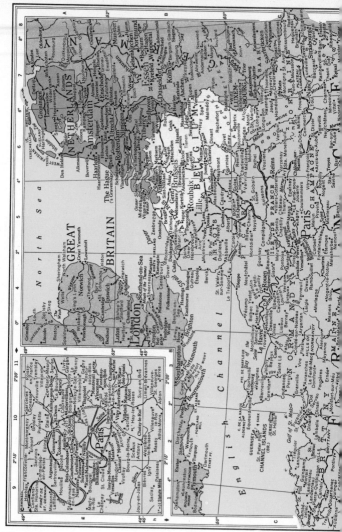

Conic Projection
SCALE 1 : 6,920,000   1 Inch = 109 Statute Miles

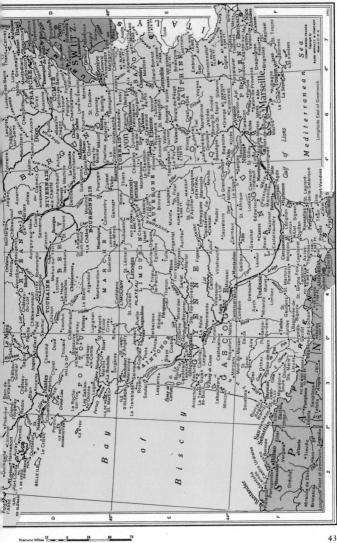

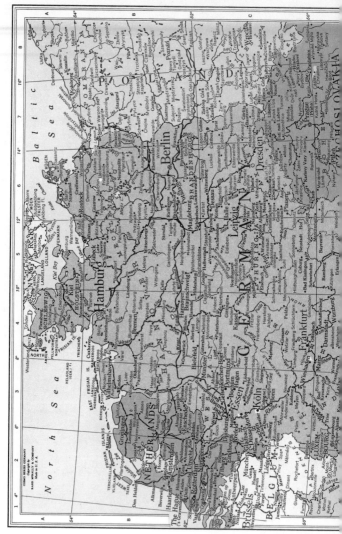

Conic Projection
SCALE 1 : 6,920,000   1 Inch = 109 Statute Miles

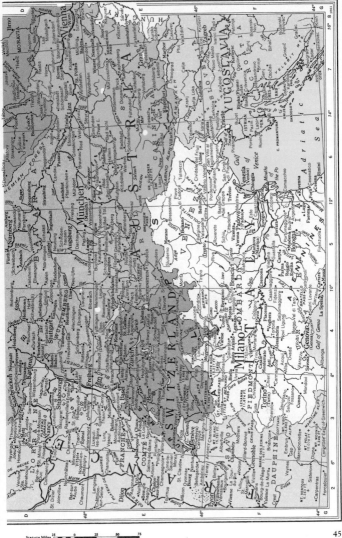

SPAIN AND PORTUGAL

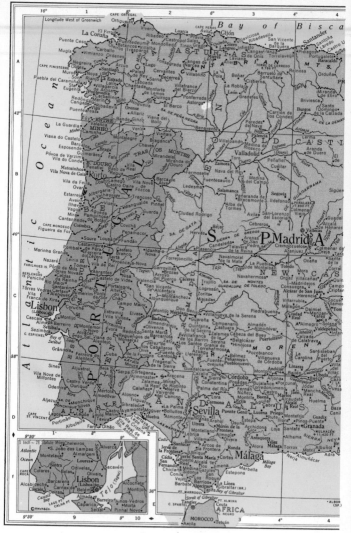

Conic Projection
SCALE 1 : 6,920,000   1 Inch = 109 Statute Miles

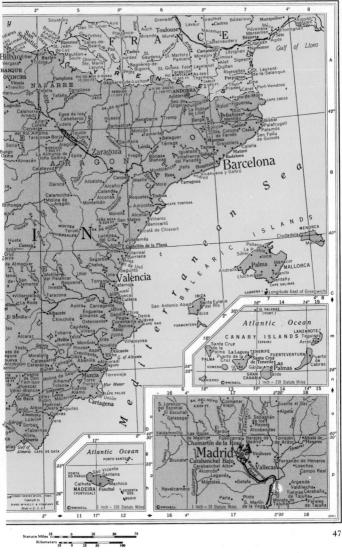

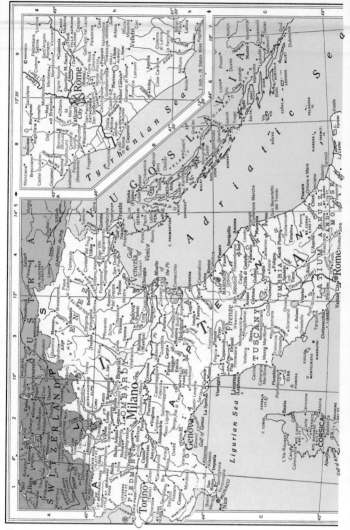

Conic Projection
SCALE 1 : 6,920,000   1 Inch = 109 Statute Miles

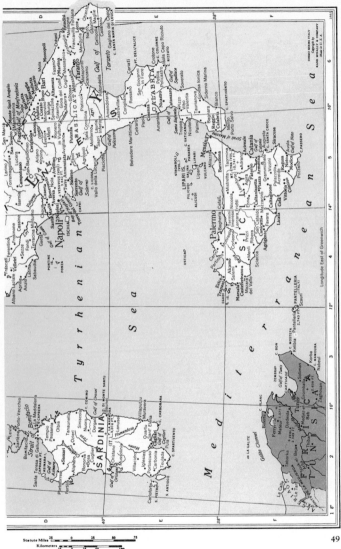

Conic Projection
SCALE 1 : 6,920,000   1 Inch = 109 Statute Miles

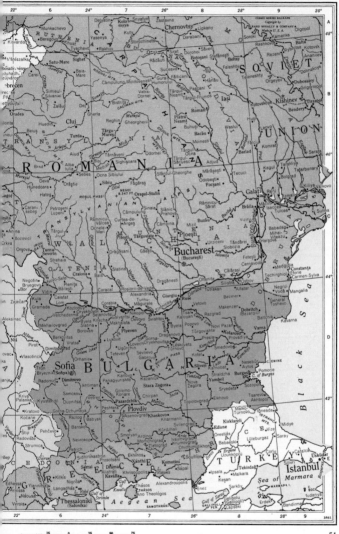

POLAND AND CZECHOSLOVAKIA

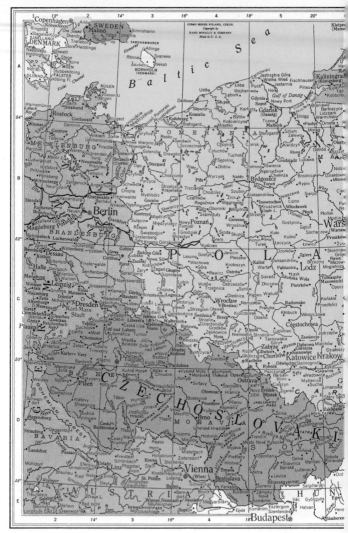

COSMO SERIES POLAND, CZECH.
Copyright by
RAND McNALLY & COMPANY
Made in U. S. A.

Conic Projection

SCALE 1 : 6,920,000   1 Inch = 109 Statute Miles

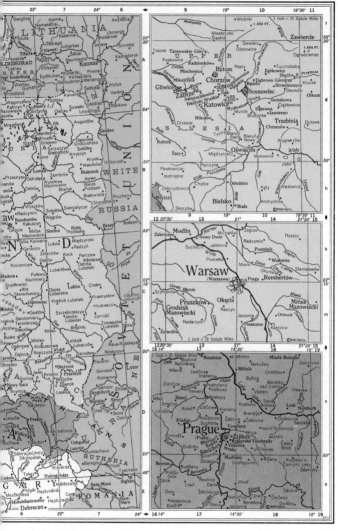

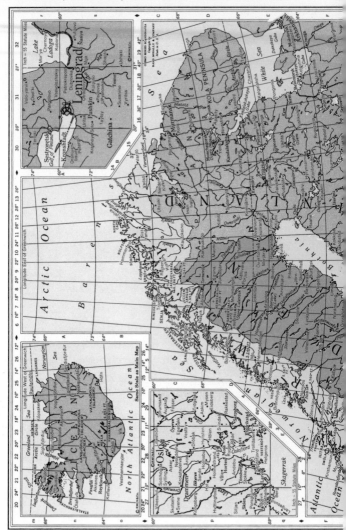

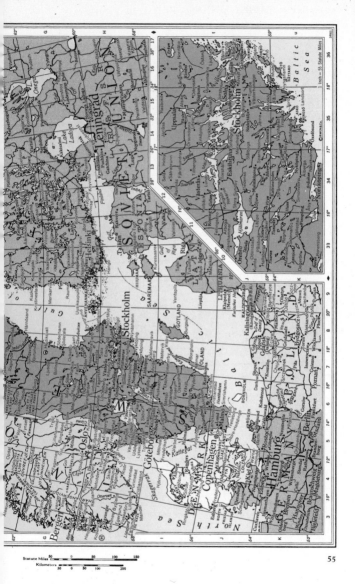

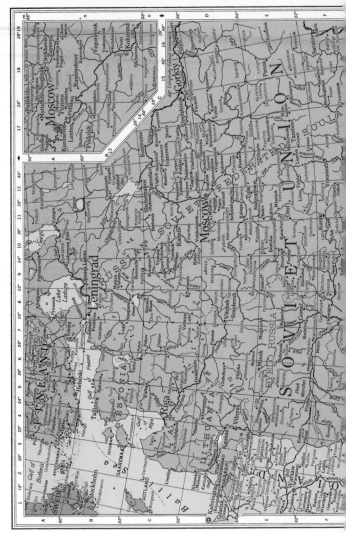

Conic Projection
SCALE 1 : 13,840,000   1 Inch = 218 Statute Miles

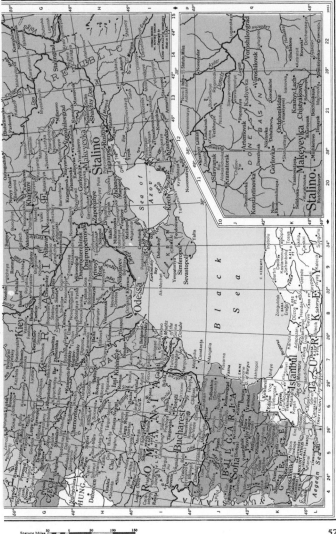

EASTERN MEDITERRANEAN

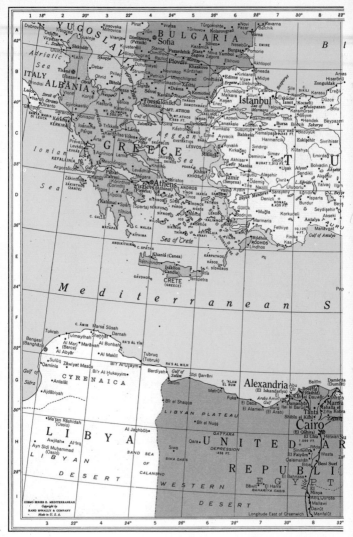

Lambert Conformal Conic Projection
SCALE 1:13,840,000   1 Inch = 218 Statute Miles

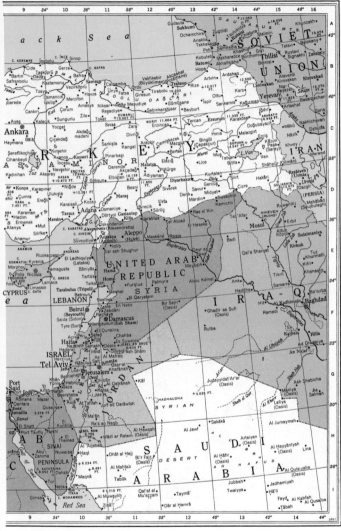

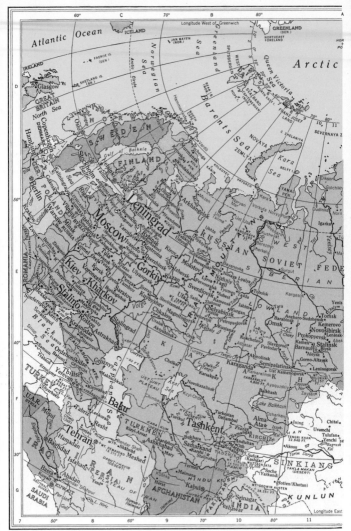

Lambert Azimuthal Equal Area Projection
SCALE 1 : 4⁹ 440,000   1 Inch ~ 764.5 Statute Miles

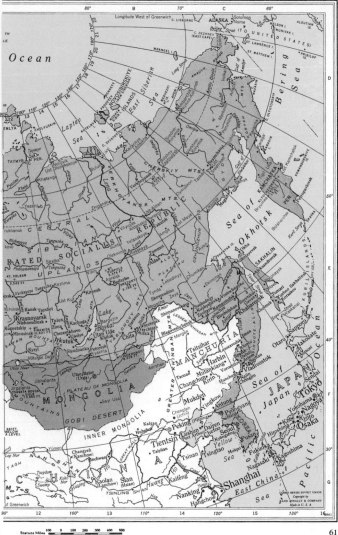

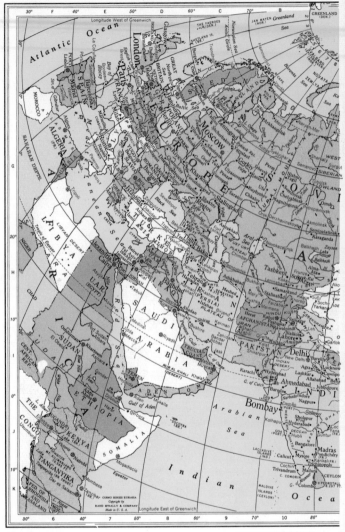

Lambert Azimuthal Equal Area Projection
SCALE 1 : 72,660,000   1 Inch = 1147 Statute Miles

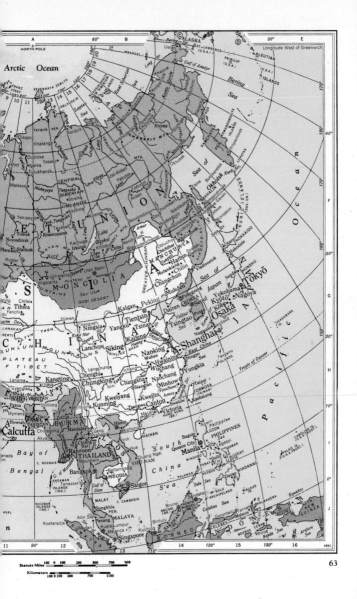

CHINA, MONGOLIA, KOREA, JAPAN AND FORMOSA

Polyconic Projection
SCALE 1:27,680,000   1 Inch=436 Statute Miles

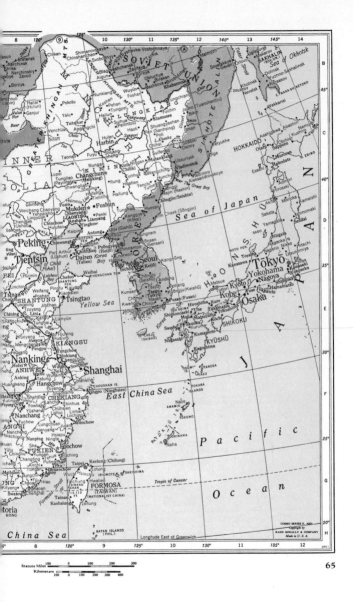

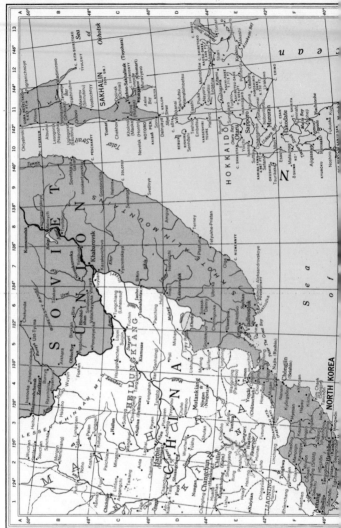

Lambert Conformal Conic Projection
SCALE 1 : 13,840,000   1 Inch = 218 Statute Miles

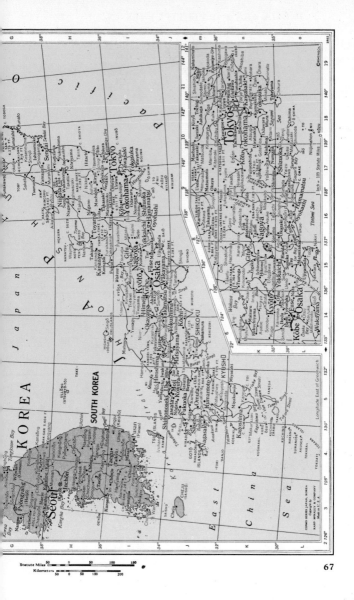

Polyconic Projection
SCALE 1 : 27,680,000   1 Inch = 436 Statute Miles

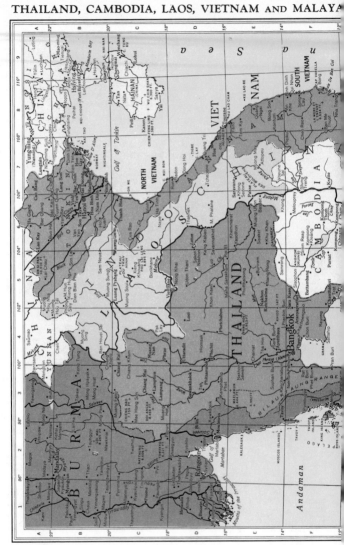

Lambert Conformal Conic Projection
SCALE 1 : 13,840,000 1 Inch = 218 Statute Miles

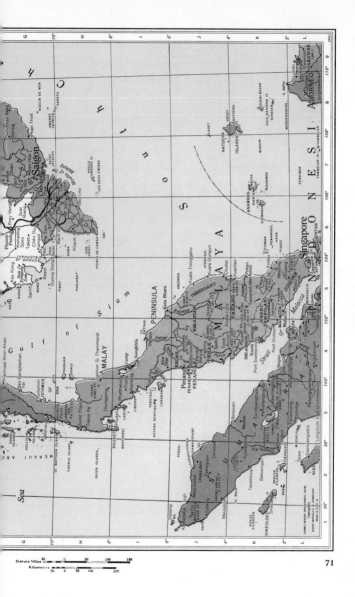

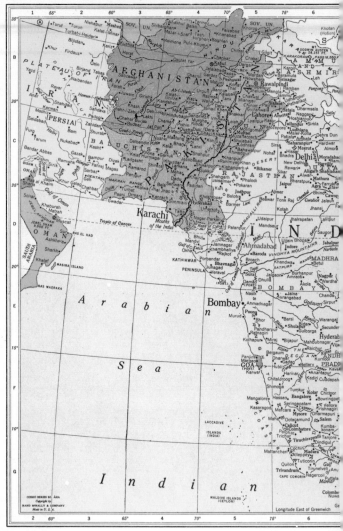

Polyconic Projection
SCALE 1 : 27,680,000   1 Inch = 436 Statute Miles

CENTRAL INDIA AND NEPAL

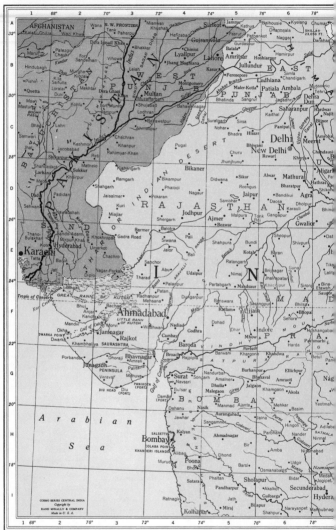

Lambert Conformal Conic Projection
SCALE 1:13,840,000   1 Inch = 218 Statute Miles

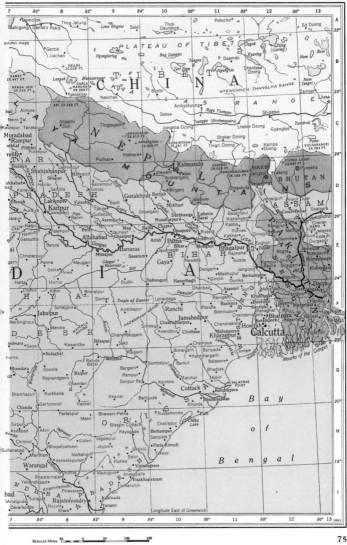

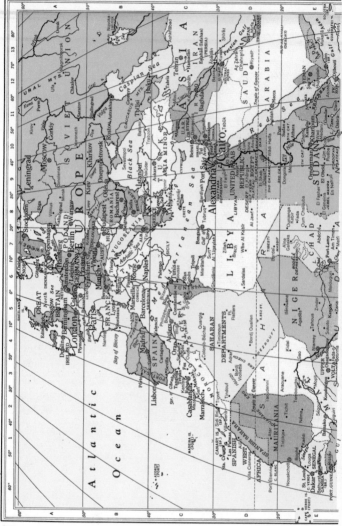

Sinusoidal Projection
SCALE 1 : 62,821,000   1 Inch=991 Statute Miles

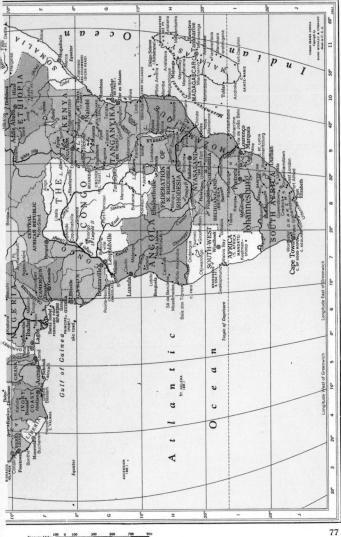

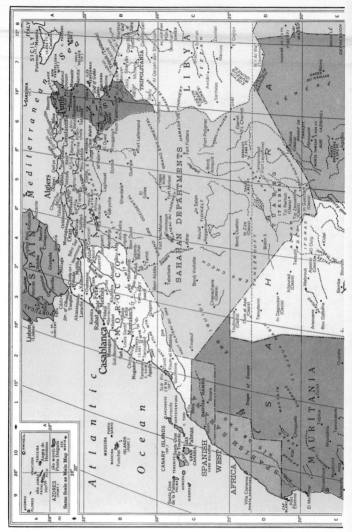

Sinusoidal Projection
SCALE 1:27,680,000 1 Inch=436 Statute Miles

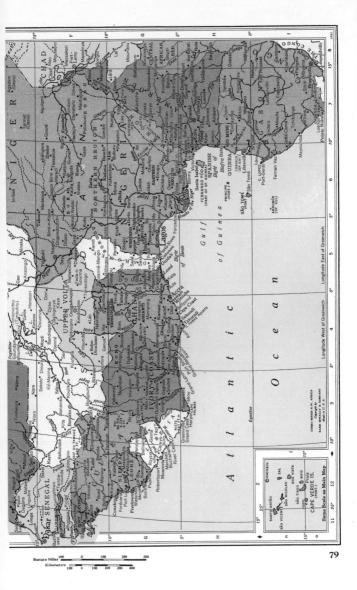

Statute Miles 100 0 100 200 300

Kilometers 100 0 100 200 300 400

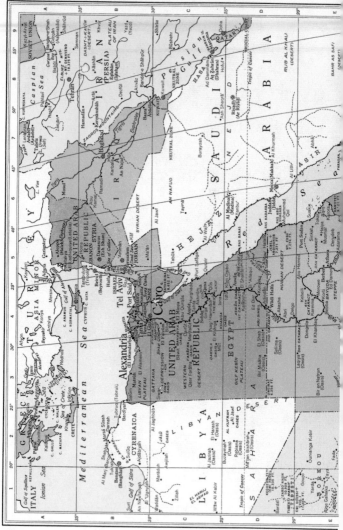

Sinusoidal Projection
SCALE 1:13,840,000   1 Inch=218 Statute Miles

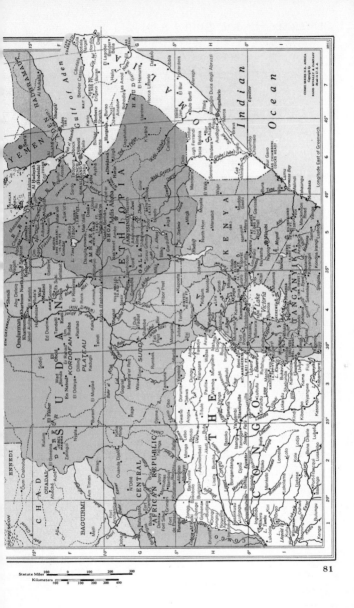

Sinusoidal Projection
SCALE 1:27,680,000   1 Inch = 436 Statute Miles

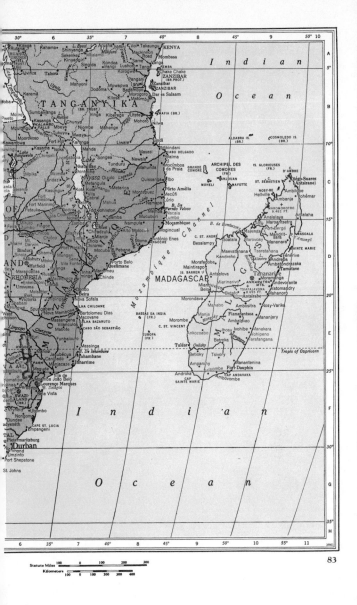

Statute Miles 100 0 100 200 300

Kilometers 100 0 100 200 300 400

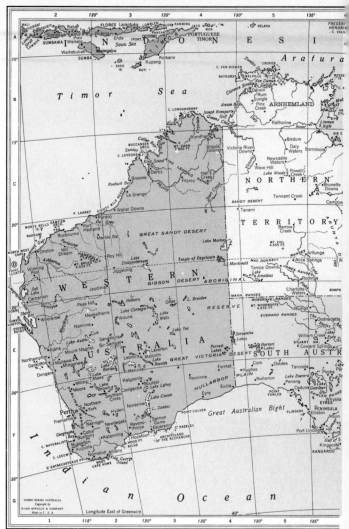

Lambert Azimuthal Equal Area Projection
SCALE 1 : 27,680,000   1 Inch = 436 Statute Miles

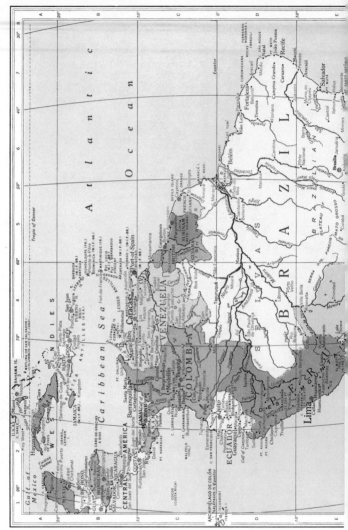

Sinusoidal Projection
SCALE 1 : 50,974,000   1 Inch = 804.5 Statute Miles

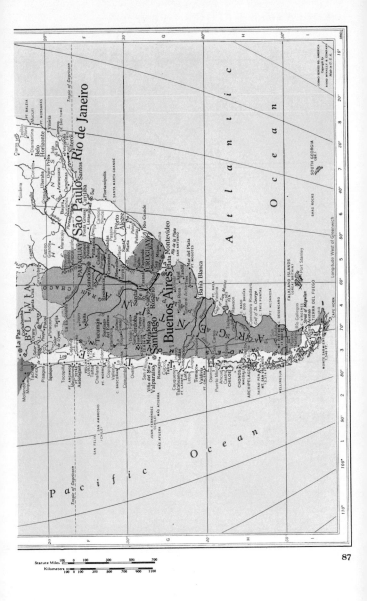

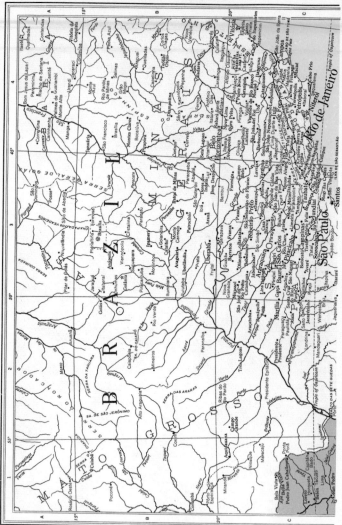

Oblique Conic Conformal Projection
SCALE 1:13,840,000   1 Inch = 218 Statute Miles

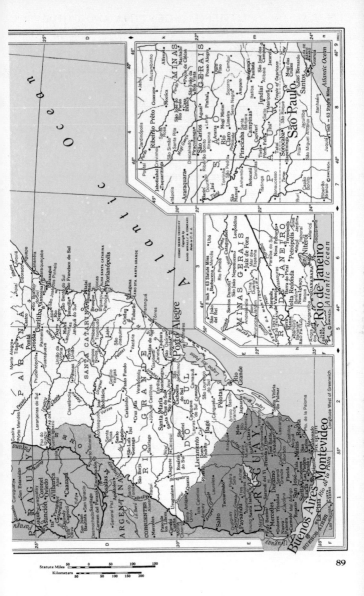

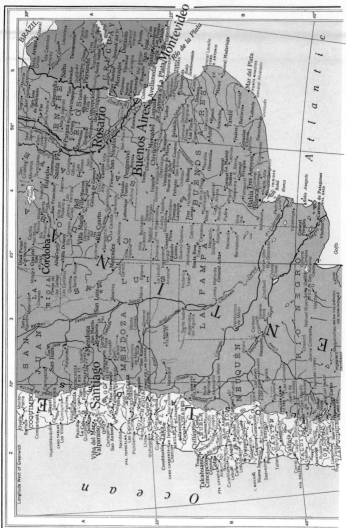

Oblique Conic Conformal Projection
SCALE 1:8,000,000   1 Inch = 126 Statute Miles

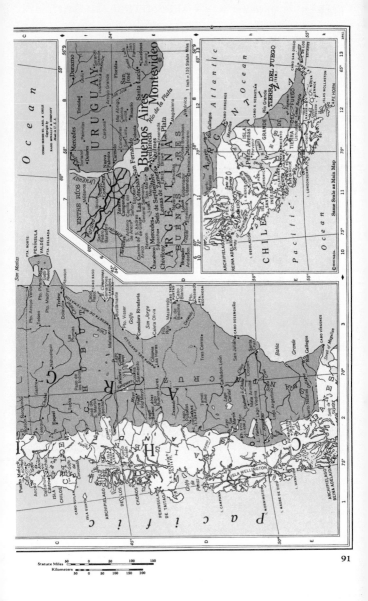

Statute Miles 50 0 50 100 150
Kilometers 50 0 50 100 150 200

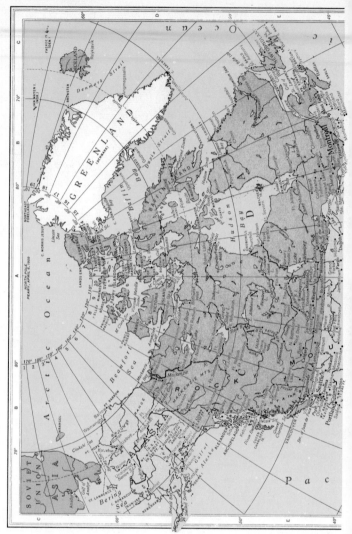

Lambert Azimuthal Equal Area Projection
SCALE 1 : 55,320,000   1 Inch = 847.5 Statute Miles

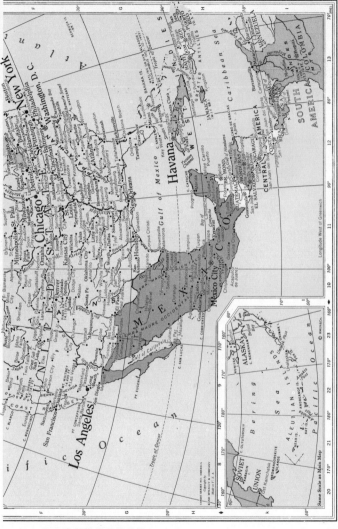

CENTRAL AMERICA

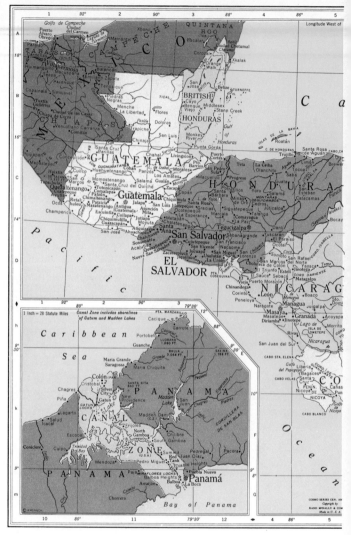

Oblique Conic Conformal Projection
SCALE 1 : 10,380,000   1 Inch = 164.5 Statute Miles

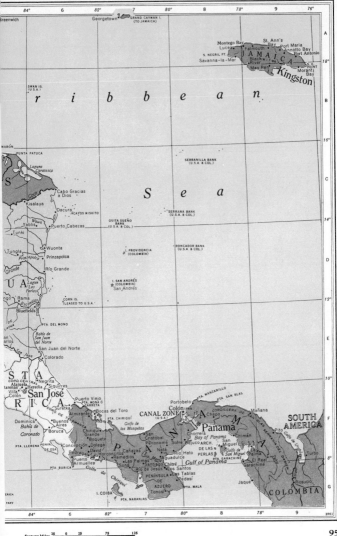

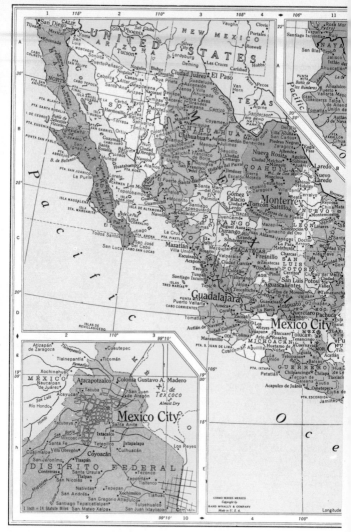

Oblique Conic Conformal Projection
SCALE 1 : 20,760,000   1 inch = 327 Statute Miles

WEST INDIES

Oblique Conic Conformal Projection
SCALE 1 : 10,380,000 1 Inch = 164.5 Statute Miles

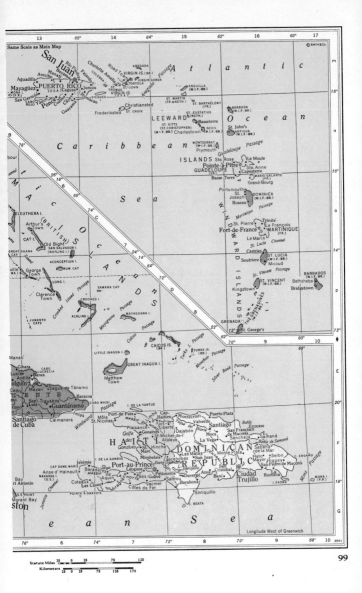

©RMN&Co.

13   66°   14   64°   15   62°   16   60°   17

A t l a n t i c

San Juan
Río Piedras
Charlotte Amalie
Road To
VIRGIN IS. (BR.)
ANEGADA
Arecibo
Manatí
Bayamón
Fajardo
VIRGIN GORDA
Anguilla Passage
ANGUILLA
(W.I.F.-BR.)
Aguadilla
MONA
PUERTO RICO
Caguas
Juncos
THOMAS ST.JOHN
TORTOLA
Mayagüez
(U.S.A.)
VIRGIN IS.
Cayey
Humacao
VIEQUES
ST. MARTIN
(FR.&NETH.)
ST. BARTHÉLEMY
(FR.)
San Germán
Coamo
ST. EUSTATIUS
(NETH.)
BARBUDA
(W.I.F.-BR.)
CABO
ROJO
Yauco
Ponce
Guayama
Christiansted
ST. CROIX
Basseterre
ST. KITTS
(ST.CHRISTOPHER)
Charlestown
ST. JOHN'S
ANTIGUA
Frederiksted
LEEWARD
NEVIS
(W.I.F.-BR.)
(W.I.F.-BR.)

O c e a n

18°

n

C a r i b b e a n

MONTSERRAT
(W.I.F.-BR.)
Plymouth

ISLANDS
Ste. Rose
Le Moule
Pointe-à-Pitre
GUADELOUPE
Ste. Anne
Capesterre
Basse-Terre
(FR.)
Guadeloupe Passage
MARIE-GALANTE
(FR.)
Grand-Bourg

76°
B
bour
16°
26°
66°
74°

S e a

Portsmouth
St. Joseph
Roseau
DOMINICA
(W.I.F.-BR.)

ELEUTHERA I.
(BRITISH)
Arthur's Town
Old Bight
ST. L. CAT I.
SAN SALVADOR I.
(WATLING I.)
CONCEPTION I.
RUM CAY

Martinique
Passage

St. Pierre
Le François
Trinité
Fort-de-France
MARTINIQUE
(FR.)
Le Marin
Micoud
St. Lucia Channel

74°

o

C

I
S
L
A
N
D
S

7
24°
14°
64°

George
Town
LONG I.
Clarence
Town
Crooked Island Passage
Samana Cay
CROOKED I.
ACKLINS
Mayaguana Passage
MAYAGUANA I.
JUMENTO
CAYS

12°

Castries
Soufrière
ST. LUCIA
(W.I.F.-BR.)
St. Vincent Passage
BARBADOS
(W.I.F.-BR.)
ST. VINCENT
(W.I.F.-BR.)
Kingstown
Bathsheba
Bridgetown

D

P

THE GRENADINES

GRENADA
St. George's
12°

70°
9
60°
10
66°

Caicos
Passage
LITTLE INAGUA I.
CAICOS IS.
(BR.)
TURKS IS.
(BR.)
Mouchoir Passage
Manatí
Gibara
CABO
LUCRECIA
Banes
GREAT INAGUA I.
Matthew
Town
Silver Bank Passage
Silver Bank

E

20°

Sta. Lucía
Antilla
Holguín
Mayarí
Sagua de Tánamo
Baracoa
CABO MAISÍ
I. DE LA TORTUE
Port-de-Paix
Cap-Haïtien
Monte Cristi
Puerto Plata
VICENTE
Cedro
San Tiburcio
San Luis
Guantánamo
Caimanera
Windward Passage
Môle
St. Nicolas
Limbé
Massif
Gonaïves
Plaisance
Valverde
Santiago
Bahía
Escocesa
Santiago
de Cuba
Imías
Baracoa
Golfe
St-Michel-de-l'
Liberté
La Vega
San Francisco
de Macorís
Sánchez
Samaná
Bahía de Samaná
HAITI
Gonaïves
St. Raphaël
Hinche
DOMINICAN
Monte Plata
Sabana
de la Mar
Las Matas
Seibo
Manati
I. DE LA GONÂVE
Mirebalais
REPUBLIC
Mata
Higüey
CABO
ENGAÑO
Jérémie
Anse d'Hainault
Baradères
MASSIF
Port-au-Prince
Pétionville
St. Juan
San Pedro de Macorís
Las Cayes
Coteaux
Aquin
Petit-Goâve
Saltrou
Azua
Baní
Ciudad
Trujillo
Romana
MONA I.
(P.R.)
CAP DAME-MARIE
Jacmel
Côtes de Fer
Barahona
Cristóbal
La Saona
Mona Passage

F

18°

NAVASSA I.
(U.S.)
POINTE À GRAVOIS
Enriquillo
CABO BEATA

G

O c e a n
S e a

Longitude West of Greenwich

76°
6
74°
7
72°
8
70°
9
68°
10

3R61

Statute Miles   25   0   25   75   125
Kilometers   25   0   25   75   125   175

CANADA

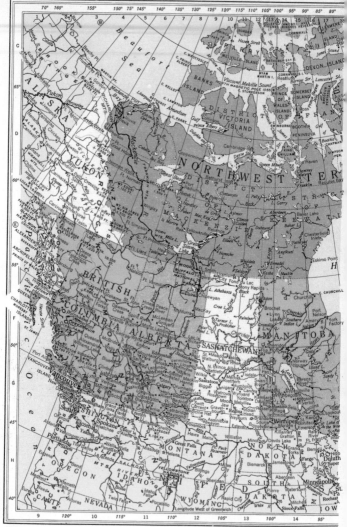

Lambert Conformal Conic Projection
SCALE 1:13,840,000   1 Inch = 218 Statute Miles

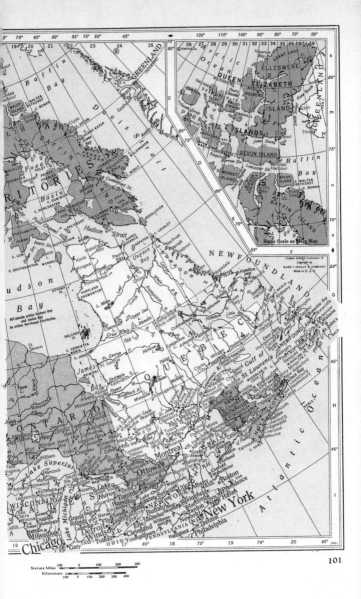

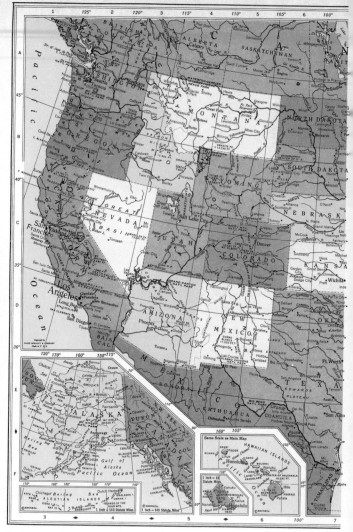

Lambert Conformal Conic Projection
SCALE 1:26,086,000   1 Inch = 411 Statute Miles

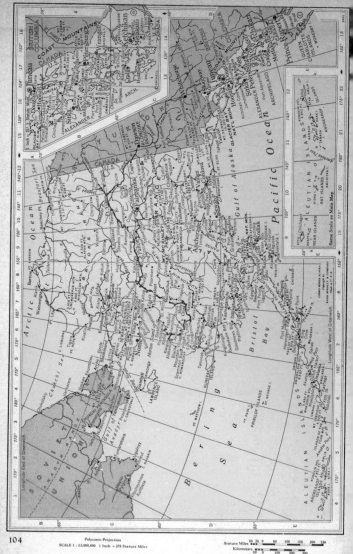

Polyconic Projection
SCALE 1 : 23,800,000   1 Inch = 375 Statute Miles

Statute Miles
Kilometers

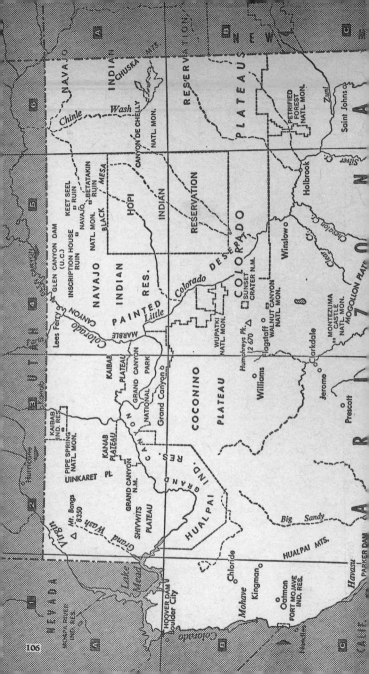

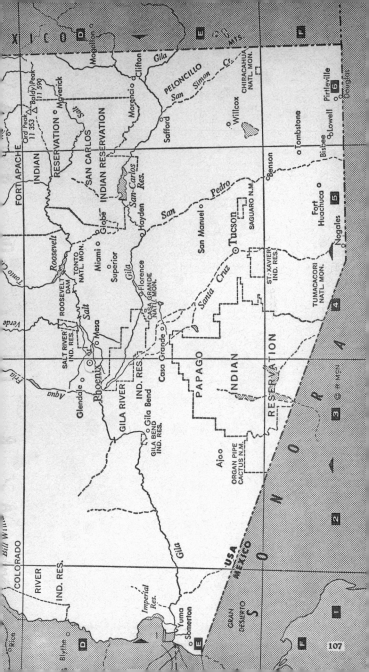

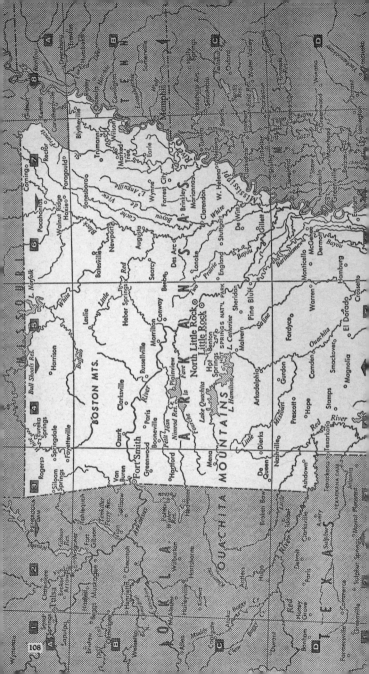

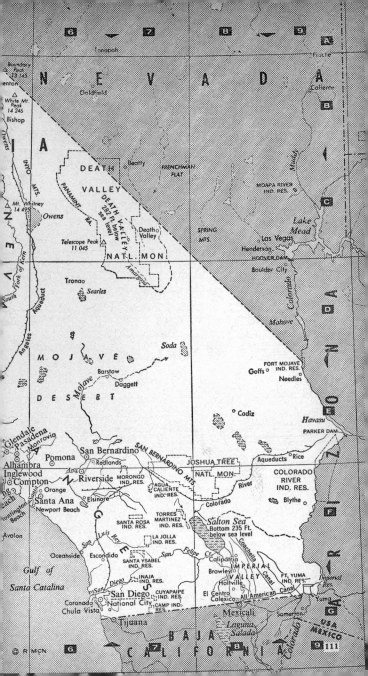

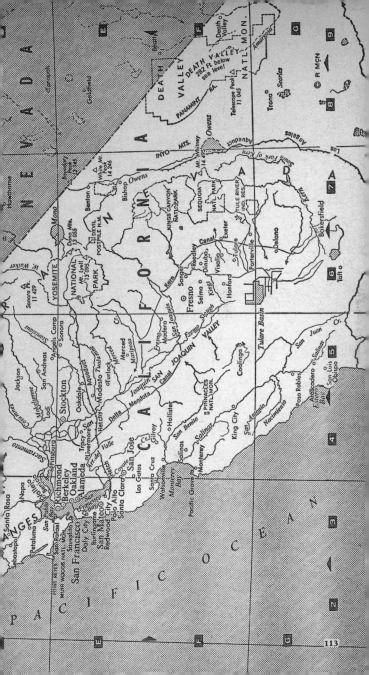

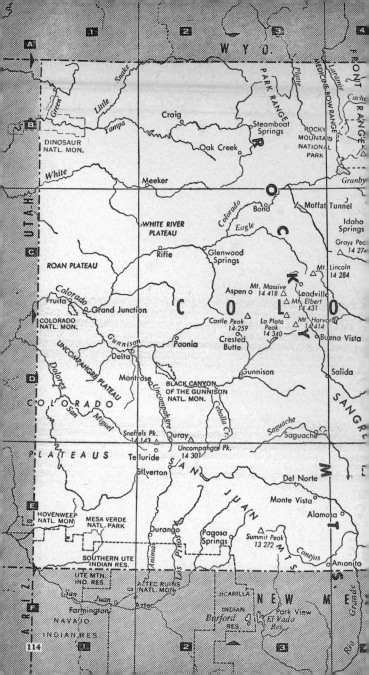

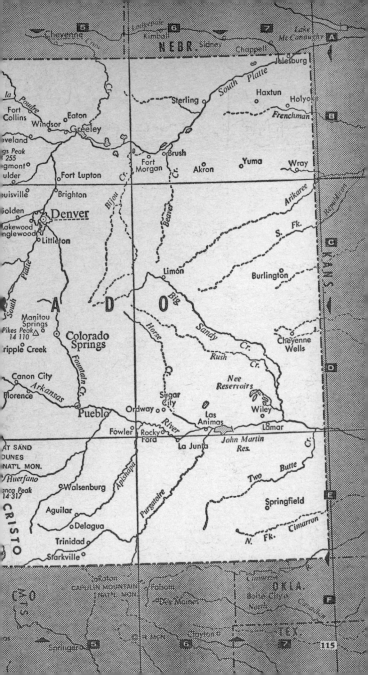

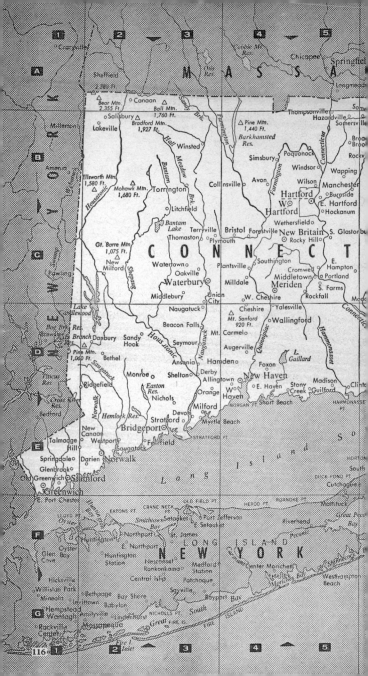

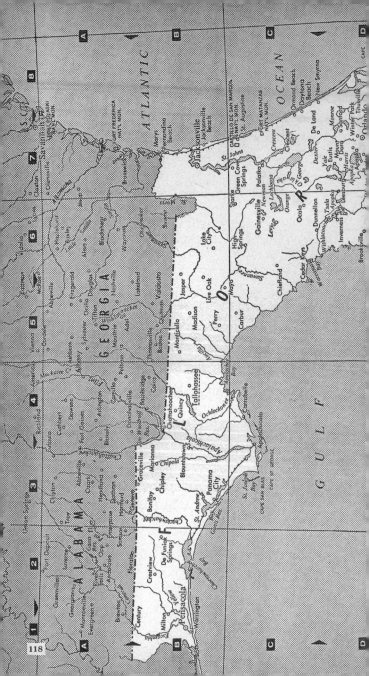

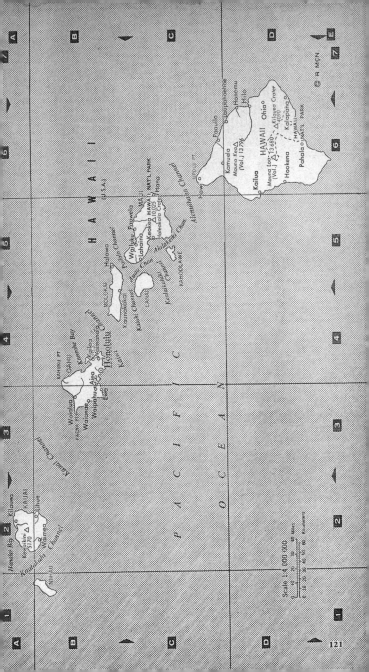

HAWAII
(U.S.A.)

KAUAI
MOLOKAI
OAHU
Honolulu
LANAI
MAUI
KAHOOLAWE
HAWAII

HAWAII NATL. PARK

P   A   C   I   F   I   C   O   C   E   A   N

Scale 1:4,000,000

121

© R MCN

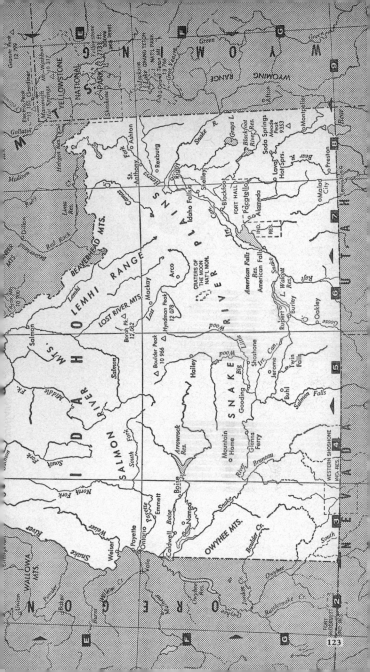

MICH.
INDIANA
KENTUCKY
OHIO
ILL.
Kalamazoo
Battle Creek
Jackson
Highland Park
Winnetka
Wilmette
Evanston
Oak Park
CHICAGO
Cicero
Benton Harbor
St. Joseph
Royalton
Decatur
Dowagiac
Vicksburg
Union City
Three Rivers
Quincy
Coldwater
Bronsona
Constantine
Sturgis
Reading
Three Oaks
Niles
Cassopolis
Buchanan
Blue Island
Harvey
Hammond
Chicago Hts.
Steger
Whiting
East Chicago
Gary
Chesterton
Michigan City
La Porte
Mishawaka
South Bend
Elkhart
Goshen
Lagrange
Angola
Montpelier
Ligonier
Kendallville
Butler
Hobart
Valparaiso
Bremen
Nappanee
Wawasee
Garrett
Auburn
Hicksville
Crown Point
Plymouth
Knox
Lowell
Culver
Warsaw
Columbia City
Maumee
New Haven
Bradley
Momence
North Judson
Rochester
Winamac
Tippecanoe
Rensselaer
Iroquois
North Manchester
Fort Wayne
Huntington
Van Wert
Monon
Kentland
Goodland
Logansport
Eel
Decatur
Wabash
Bluffton
Peru
Warren
Berne
Gilman
Watseka
Monticello
Montpelier
Mississinewa
Hoopeston
Fowler
Delphi
Kokomo
Marion
Hartford City
Flora
Gas City
Portland
West Lafayette
La Fayette
Fairmount
Rantoul
Wabash
Elwood
Alexandria
Dunkirk
Frankfort
Tipton
Muncie
Winchester
Covington
Danville
Urbana
Westville
Georgetown
Veedersburg
Thorntown
Noblesville
Anderson
Union City
Crawfordsville
Lebanon
Fortville
Hagerstown
Indianapolis
Sugar
Newcastle
Richmond
Eaton
Greenfield
Cambridge City
Rockville
Danville
Beech Grove
Knightstown
Clinton
Greencastle
Rushville
Liberty
Paris
Universal
Greenwood
Connersville
Brazil
Harmony
Mooresville
Shelbyville
Hamilton
West Terre Haute
Terre Haute
Franklin
Brookville
Marshall
Martinsville
Greensburg
Casey
Spencer
Edinburg
Cincinnati
Farmersburg
Columbus
Hymera
Jasonville
White
Lawrenceburg
Shelburn
Bloomington
Osgood
Covington
Linton
Robinson
Sullivan
Worthington
North Vernon
Vernon
Dugger
Fork
Rising Sun
Bloomfield
Seymour
Bedford
Brownstown
Vevay
East
Lawrenceville
Bicknell
Loogootee
Madison
Vincennes
Mitchell
River
Carrollton
Owenton
Bridgeport
Shoals
Orleans
Scottsburg
Washington
Paoli
Salem
French Lick
Mount Carmel
Petersburg
La Grange
Eminence
Patoka
Kentucky
Jeffersonville
St. Matthews
Princeton
Jasper
Oakland City
English
New Albany
Louisville
Frankfort
Owensville
Huntingburg
Fort Branch
Corydon
Oakdale
Ohio
Shelbyville
Lexington
New Harmony
Versailles
Boonville
Evansville
Wabash
Newburgh
Tell City
Cannelton
Lawrenceburg
Mt. Vernon
Hawesville
Bardstown
Henderson
Rockport
Cloverport
Harrodsburg
Corydon
Owensboro
Elizabethtown
Springfield
Morganfield
Sturgis
Sebree
Lebanon
Livermore
Hodgenville
Hartford
Clay
Leitchfield
A
B
C
D
E
F
1
2
3
4
5

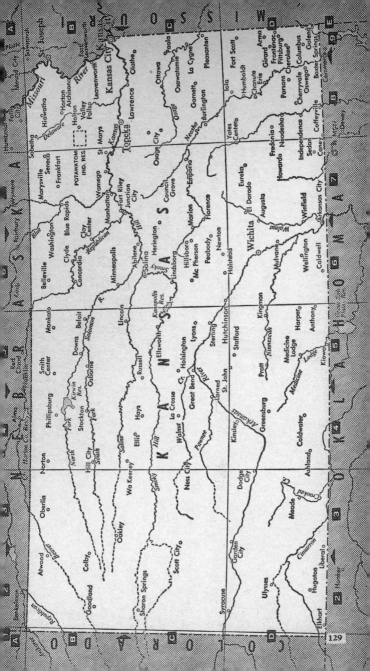

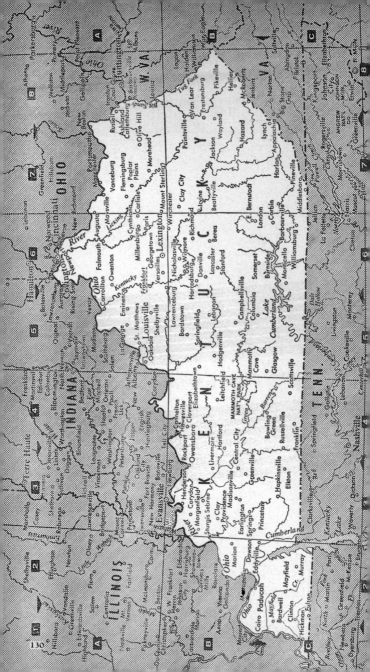

130

GOVERNMENT BUILDINGS AND POINTS OF INTEREST

1. The Capitol
2. White House
3. Commerce Department
4. Post Office
5. Internal Revenue Bureau
6. Justice Department
7. Archives
8. Federal Trade Commission
9. Unemployment Compensation
10. Municipal Building
11. Judiciary Sq. (Municipal Court, Police Court, Juvenile Court, Court of Appeals)
12. Accounting Office
13. Civil Service Commission
14. Lincoln Museum
15. Peterson House
16. Treasury Department
17. Octagon House
18. Court of Claims
19. Interior Department Buildings
20. General Services Adm. Building
21. State Department
22. Navy Department
23. National Academy of Sciences
24. Federal Reserve Board
25. Public Health Service
26. Pan American Union

27. Lincoln Memorial
28. Washington Monument
29. National Museum
30. National Art Gallery
31. Senate Office Buildings
32. Government Printing Office
33. Post Office
34. Union Station
35. Supreme Court
36. Library of Congress and Annex
37. House Office Buildings
38. Botanic Gardens
39. Health, Education, Welfare Department
40. Railroad Retirement Board Building
41. F.B.I. Identification Division
42. Army Institute of Pathology
43. Arts Industries Building
44. Museums
45. Department of Agriculture
46. Bureau of Engraving and Printing
47. Capitol Heating and Power Plant
48. Federal Warehouse
49. Federal Office Building
50. Thomas Jefferson National Memorial
51. Marine Barracks
52. Smithsonian Institution
53. Tariff Commission

133

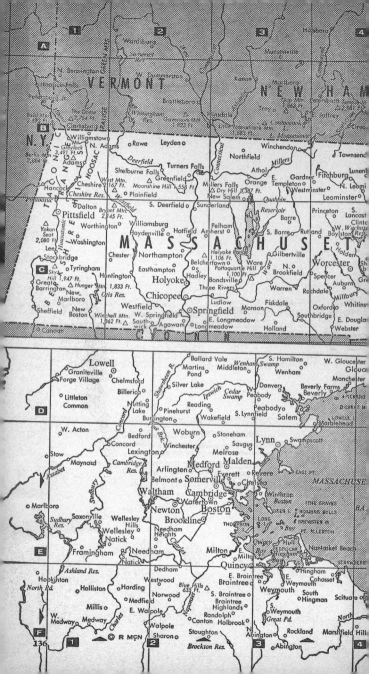

ATLANTIC OCEAN

MASSACHUSETTS BAY

CAPE COD BAY

CAPE COD

NANTUCKET SOUND

MARTHA'S VINEYARD

NANTUCKET ISLAND

New Market · Portsmouth · Kittery Point

Manchester · Exeter · Hampton

Amesbury · Newburyport

Haverhill · W. Newbury · Georgetown · PLUM I.

Salem · Merrimac · Ipswich · HALIBUT PT.

Methuen · Lawrence · Andover · Ipswich · Gloucester

Lowell · Ballard Vale · S. Hamilton · Beverly

Billerica · Wilmington · Danvers · Marblehead

Chelmsford · W. Reading · Peabody · Salem · Swampscott

Concord · Woburn · Melrose · Lynn

Concord · Medford · Somerville · Chelsea · Winthrop

Waltham · Cambridge · Boston · Boston Bay

Newton · Brookline · PT. ALLERTON

Wellesley · Natick · Milton · Hingham · Nantasket Beach · STRAWBERRY PT.

Dedham · Quincy · Cohasset · Scituate

Norwood · Braintree · Randolph · Weymouth · S. Weymouth

Walpole · Canton · Holbrook · Rockland

Medway · Sharono · Stoughton · Whitman · Duxbury

Franklin · Brockton · E. Bridgewater · South Duxbury

Wrentham · Foxboro · Mansfield · Bridgewater · N. Plymouth · Plymouth · GURNET PT. · Plymouth Bay

W. Bridgewater · Manomet

N. Attleboro · Raynham · MONOMOY PT.

Attleboro Falls · Taunton · Middleboro

S. Attleboro · E. Taunton · S. Carver

Pawtucket · Assonet · Assawompset Pd.

Providence · Somerset · Long Pd. · Wareham · Cape Cod Canal · Buzzards Bay · Barnstable · Yarmouth

E. Providence · N. Swansea · Swansea · Long Plains · Mattapoisett · Hyannis · W. Yarmouth · Chatham

Cranston · Fall River · N. Westport · Fairhaven · Mashpee

R.I. · Tiverton · New Bedford · S. Dartmouth · Falmouth

Newport · N. Dartmouth · Dartmouth · Buzzards Bay · NANTUCKET SOUND

BRENTON PT. · SAKONNET · NASHAWENA · ELIZABETH ISLAND · Oak Bluffs

PT. JUDITH · CUTTYHUNK · PASQUE · Vineyard Haven · CHAPPAQUIDDICK · MUSKEGET I. · TUCKERNUCK I.

GAY HEAD · Edgartown · Nantucket

Gay Head · MARTHA'S VINEYARD · SMITH PT. · NANTUCKET ISLAND

SQUIBNOCKET PT. · NO MANS LAND

HIRE · Sandown · Derry · Hudson · Pepperell · Dracut · Marlboro · Hudson · Hopkinton · Medway

© R McN

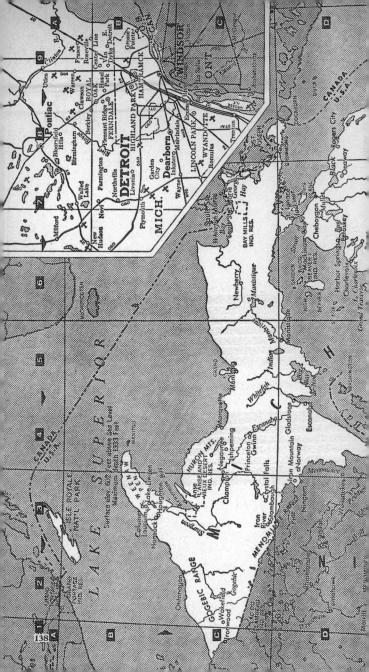

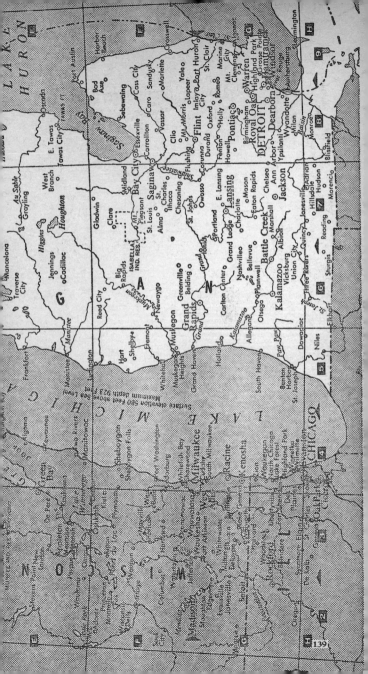

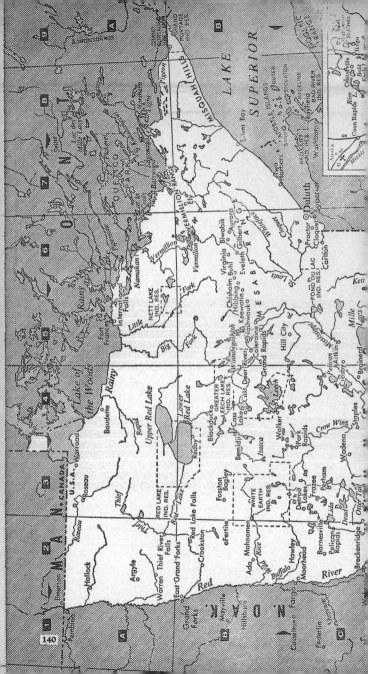

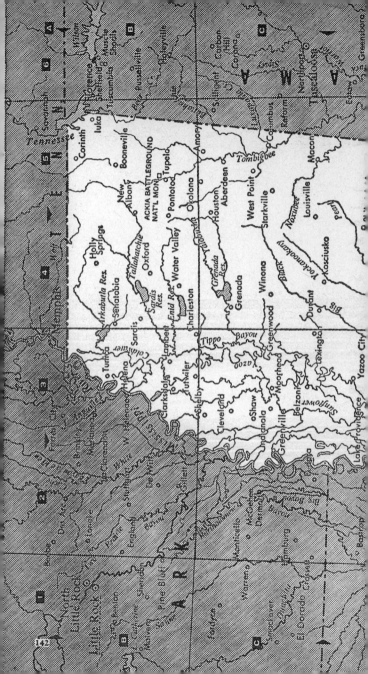

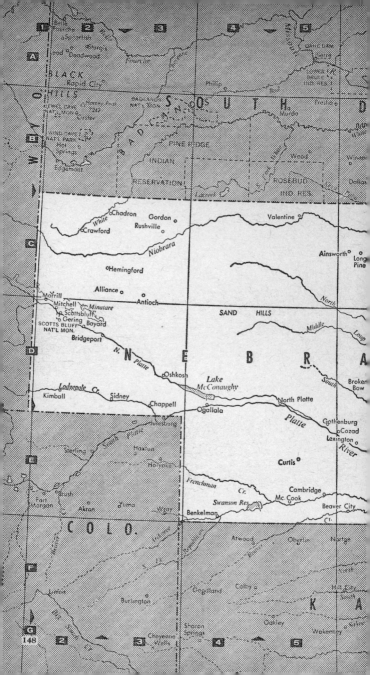

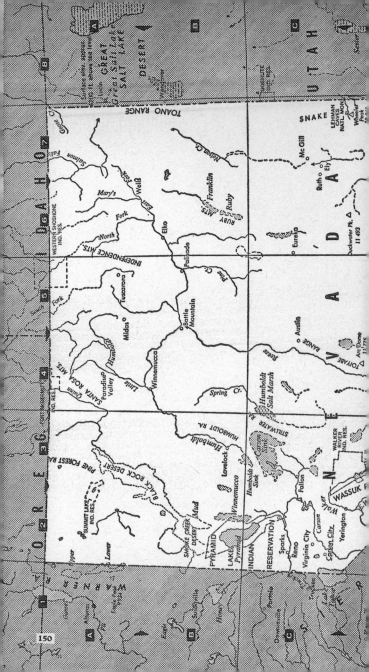

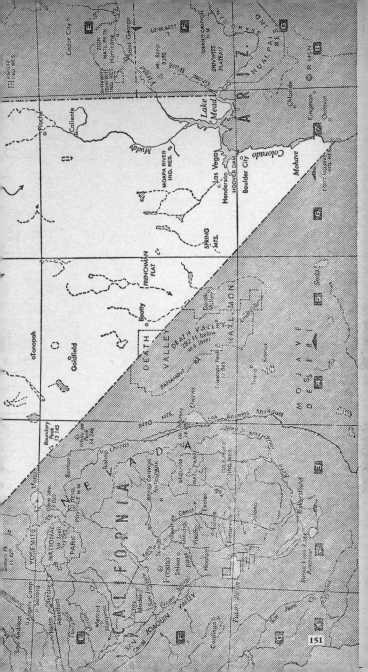

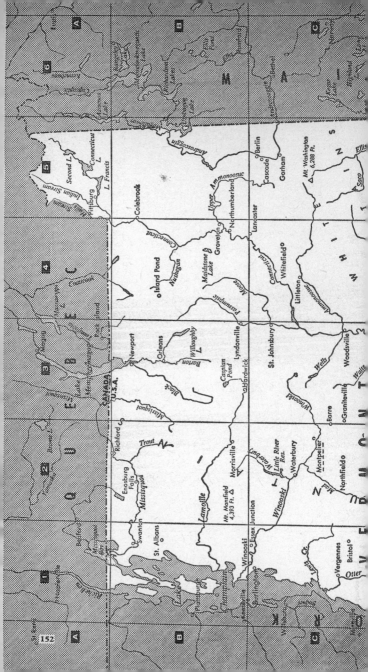

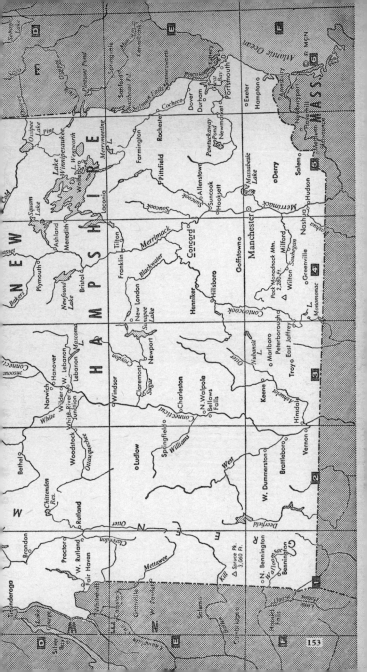

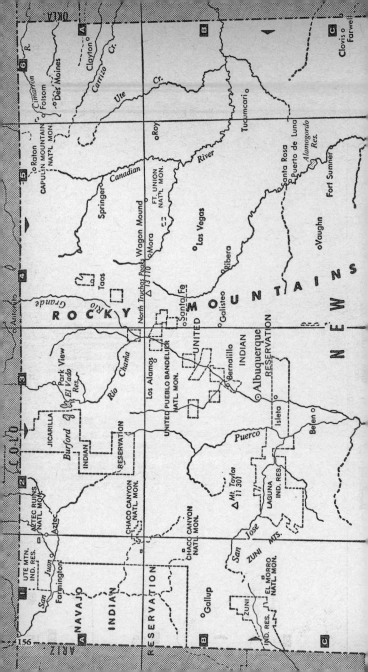

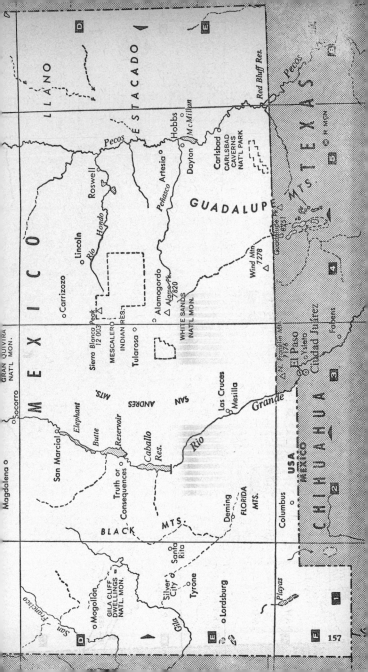

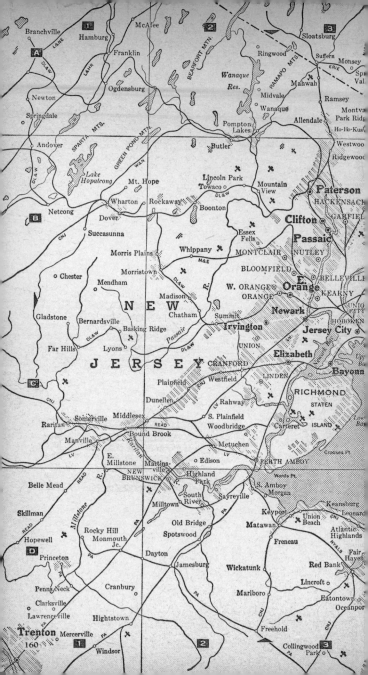

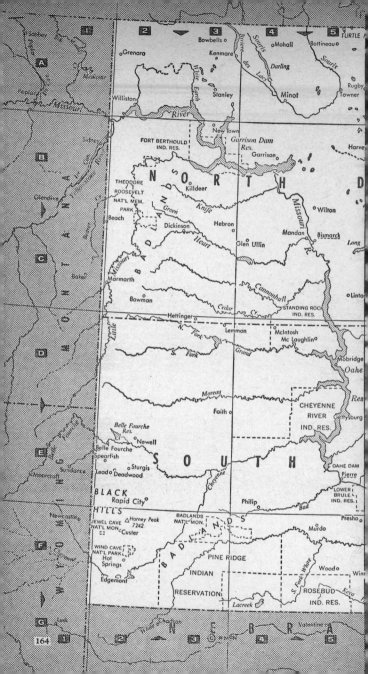

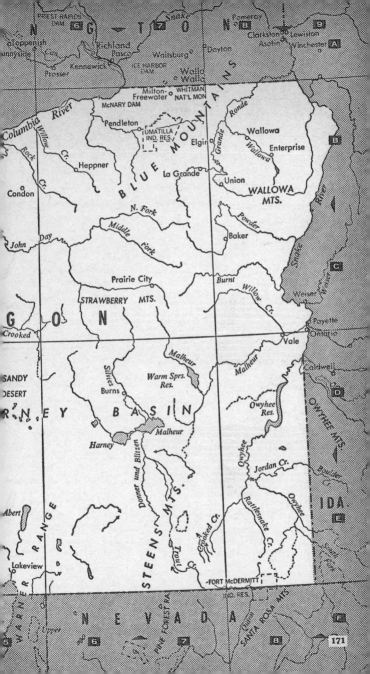

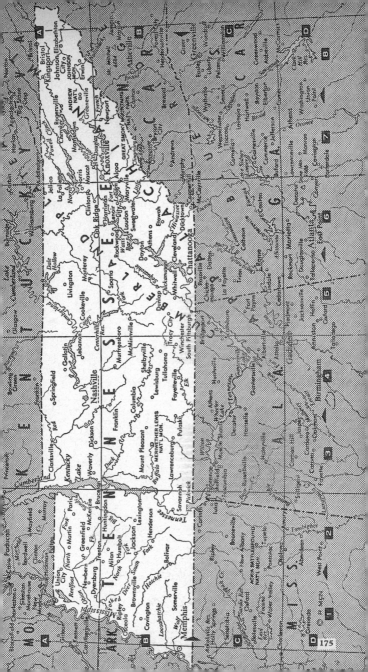

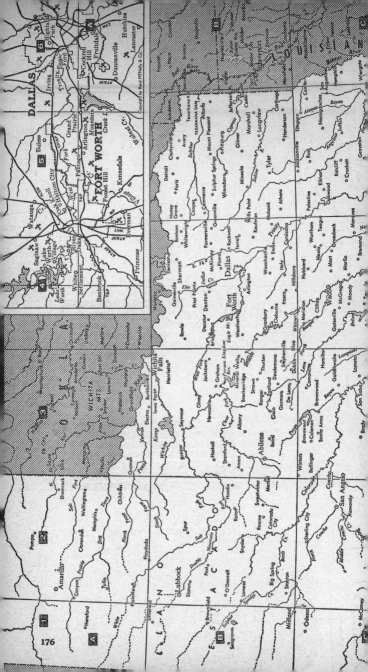

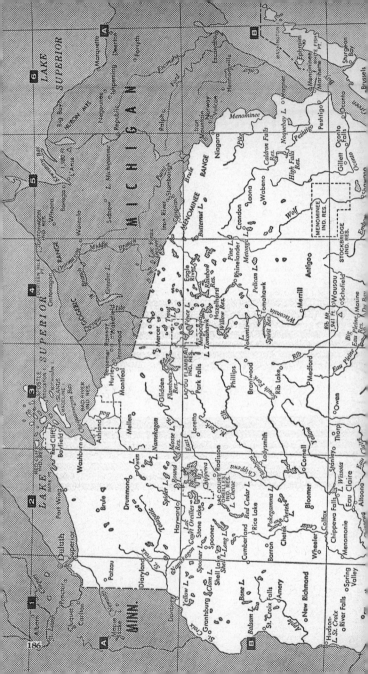

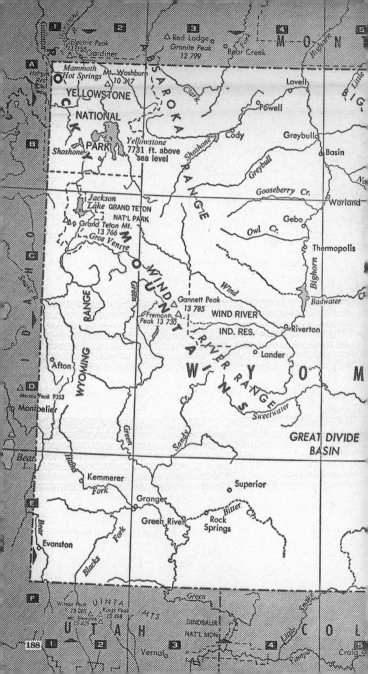

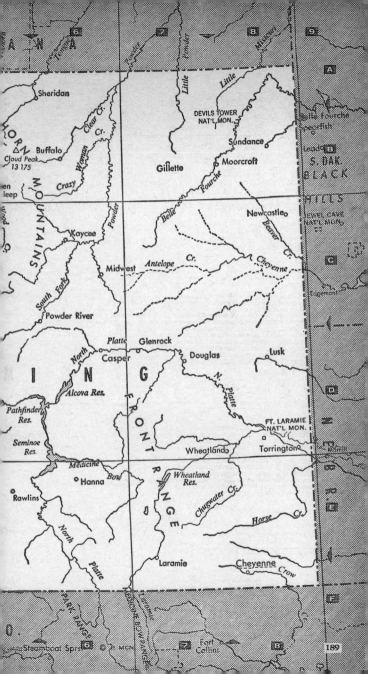

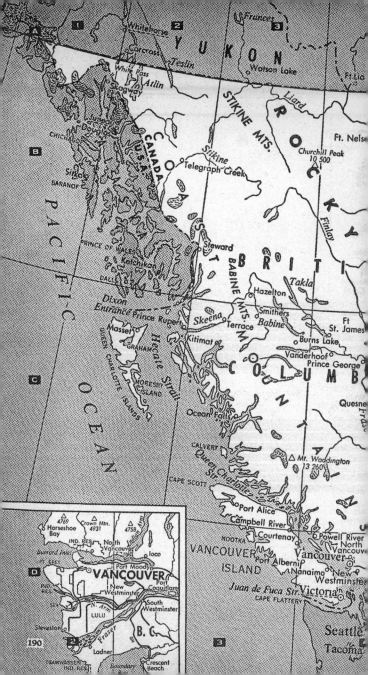

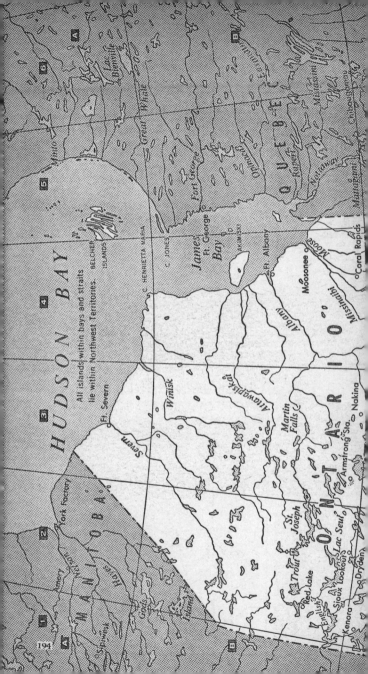

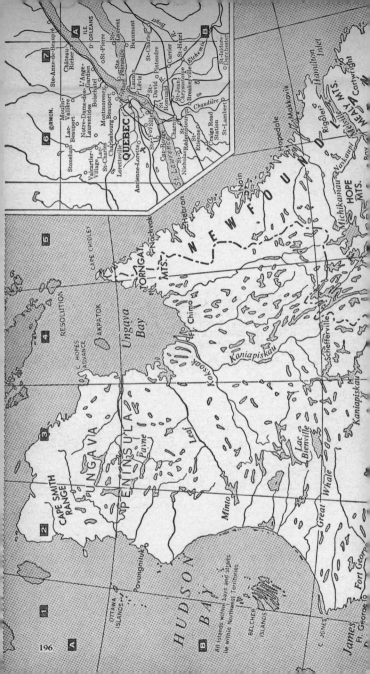

GULF OF ST. LAWRENCE

CAPE GASPÉ

NEWFOUNDLAND

C. ANGUILLE

C. RAY

Cabot Strait

BRION

BIRD ROCK

Cap-Aux-Meules

MAGDALEN ISLANDS (Que.)

ST. PAUL I.

CAPE NORTH

Aspy Bay

Tignish

Alberton

Leary

Sta. L

Malpeque Bay

PRINCE EDWARD ISLAND

PRINCE EDWARD ISLAND NAT'L PARK

CAPE BRETON HIGHLANDS NAT'L PARK

St. Anns Bay

Waterford

Sydney Mines

N. Sydney

New Dominion

Glace Bay

Summerside

Mount Stewart

Souris East

Inverness

Port Elgin

B. Verte

Charlottetown

Montague

Georgetown

Murray Harbour

L. Ainslie

Port Hood

Sydney

St. Andrew Channel

Louisbourg

CAPE BRETON ISLAND

Bras d'Or Lake

Strait of Canso

Amherst

Oxford

Pictou

Trenton

Antigonish

George Bay

Havre Boucher

Port Hawkesbury

St. Peters

Springhill

Westville

Stellarton

New Glasgow

Mulgrave

Arichat

L'ARDOISE

MADAME

Londonderry

Truro

Guysborough

Chedabucto Bay

Canso

CAPE CANSO

Cobequid Bay

Stewiacke

NOVA SCOTIA

Hantsport

Windsor

Dartmouth

Halifax

Halifax Harbour

Margaret Bay

Mahone Bay

ATLANTIC OCEAN

SABLE I. (N.S.)

© R McN

199

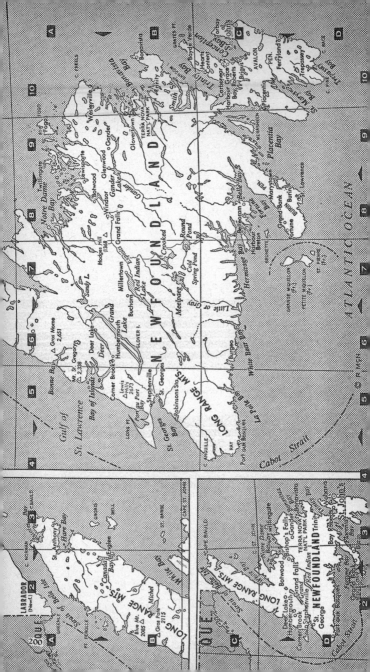

ALTITUDES OF SELECTED WORLD CITIES

Heights are given in feet.

Aachen, Ger.	580
Addis Ababa, Eth.	8,000
Albany, N.Y., U.S.	20
Albuquerque, N. Mex., U.S.	4,920
Amman, Jordan	2,400
Andorra, Andorra	3,425
Ankara, Turkey	2,250
Asheville, N.C., U.S.	1,985
Astrakhan, Sov. Un.	−50
Asunción, Par.	253
Athens (Athinai), Greece	300
Atlanta, Ga., U.S.	1,050
Baghdad, Iraq	125
Baku, Sov. Un.	−40
Banaras (Benares), India	255
Banff, Canada	4,537
Bangalore, India	3,100
Bangkok, Thailand	40
Belgrade (Beograd), Yugoslavia	450
Berlin, Ger.	115
Bern, Switz.	1,788
Birmingham, Eng.	400
Birmingham, Ala., U.S.	600
Bogotá, Colombia	8,630
Boston, Mass., U.S.	21
Bradford, Eng.	635
Brasília, Brazil	3,075
Bristol, Eng.	190
Brussels (Bruxelles), Bel.	190
Bucharest (Bucuresti), Romania	276
Budapest, Hungary	450
Buenos Aires, Arg.	45
Garmisch-Partenkirchen, Ger.	2,330
Gartok, Tibet, China	14,240
Genève (Geneva), Switz.	1,346
Glasgow, Scotland	300
Granada, Spain	2,195
Graz, Aus	1,170
Grenoble, France	770
Guadalajara, Mex.	5,051
Guatemala, Guat.	4,850
Hankow, China	150
Hanoi, Vietnam	200
Harbin, China	530
Hartford, Conn., U.S.	40
Hot Springs, Ark., U.S.	607
Houston, Tex., U.S.	40
Hyderabad, India	1,740
Indianapolis, Ind., U.S.	710
Innsbruck, Aus.	2,900
Iquitos, Peru	350
Irkutsk, Sov. Un.	1,600
Jerusalem, Israel-Jordan	2,500
Jiachan, Tibet, China	15,870
Johannesburg, S. Afr.	5,689
Kabul, Afg.	7,280
Kansas City, Mo., U.S.	750
Katmandu, Nepal	4,223
Kharkov, Sov. Un.	350
Khartoum, Sud	1,252
Kiev, Sov. Un	460
Knoxville, Tenn., U.S.	890
Krakow, Poland	800
Kyoto, Japan	360
Lahore, Pakistan	706
Lanchow, China	7,040
Omaha, Nebr., U.S.	1,040
Omsk, Sov. Un.	285
Oruro, Bolivia	12,122
Osaka, Japan	50
Ottawa, Canada	214
Paris, France	300
Peiping (Peking), China	600
Philadelphia, Pa., U.S.	100
Phoenix, Ariz., U.S.	1,090
Pittsburgh, Pa., U.S.	745
Poona, India	1,700
Portland, Oreg., U.S.	75
Potosí, Bolivia	13,600
Poznań (Posen), Poland	175
Prague (Praha), Czech.	575
Pretoria, S. Afr.	4,472
Providence, R.I., U.S.	80
Puno, Peru	12,648
Quebec, Canada	150
Quito, Ecuador	9,300
Rangoon, Burma	100
Reno, Nevada, U.S.	4,490
Rome (Roma), Italy	95
Saint Etienne, France	1,800
Saint Louis, Mo., U.S.	455
Saint Moritz, Switz.	6,037
Salisbury, Rhodesia	4,700
Salt Lake City, Utah, U.S.	4,390
San Francisco, Calif., U.S.	65
San José, Costa Rica	3,868
San Salvador, El Salvador	2,178
Santa Fe, N. Mex., U.S.	6,950
Santiago, Chile	1,800
Seattle, Wash., U.S.	75

Buffalo, N. Y., U. S. 585	La Paz, Bolivia. 12,200	Seoul (Keijo), Korea. 250
Cairo, Eg., U. A. R. 98	Leadville, Colo., U. S. 10,190	Simla, India. 7,186
Calcutta, India. 85	Leipzig, Ger. 350	Sodom, Israel. . . . . . −1,286
Canberra, Austl. 2,000	Leningrad, Sov. Un. 25	Sofia (Sofija), Bulgaria. 1,700
Canton, China. 50	Léopoldville, Bel. Cong. 1,045	Spokane, Wash., U. S. 1,890
Caracus, Ven. 3,164	Lhasa, Tibet, China. 11,800	Stalingrad, Sov. Un. 75
Cerro de Pasco, Peru. 14,385	Lille, France. 120	Stockholm, Sweden. 35
Chengtu, China. 2,700	Lima, Peru. 501	Sun Valley, Idaho, U. S. 6,000
Chicago, Ill., U. S. 595	Lisbon (Lisboa), Portugal. 285	Tabriz, Iran. 4,500
Chihuahua, Mex. 4,635	Liverpool, Eng. 130	Tacoma, Wash., U. S. 110
Chungking, China. 755	London, Eng. 245	Tananarive, Malag. 4,200
Cleveland, Ohio, U. S. 580	Los Angeles, Calif., U. S. 340	Tehran, Iran. 4,000
Cochabamba, Bolivia. 8,435	Louisville, Ky., U. S. 450	The Hague ('s Gravenhage), Neth. 5
Cody, Wyo., U. S. 4,980	Luxembourg, Lux. 1,200	Tokyo, Japan. 30
Constantine, Algeria. 2,170	Lyon, France. 770	Toronto, Canada. 254
Córdoba, Arg. 1,240	Madrid, Spain. 2,150	Tours, France. 165
Cuiabá, Brazil. 771	Managua, Nicaragua. 150	Tucson Ariz., U. S. 2,390
Cusco (Cuzco), Peru. 11,440	Manchester, Eng. 275	Tulsa, Okla., U. S. 804
Dacca, Pakistan. 70	Marrakech, Morocco. 1,600	Ulan Bator, Mongolia. 4,160
Dallas, Texas, U. S. 435	Medellín, Colombia. 4,880	Vancouver, Canada. 38
Damascus (Damas), Syr., U. A. R. 2,250	Memphis, Tenn., U. S. 275	Vienna (Wien), Aus. 550
Danzig, see Gdansk, Poland	Mexico City, Mex. 7,349	Vladivostok, Sov. Un. 100
Darjeeling, India. 6,982	Milano (Milan), Italy. 400	Warsaw (Warszawa), Poland. 240
Delhi, India. 770	Milwaukee, Wis., U. S. 635	Washington, D. C., U. S. 25
Denver, Colo., U. S. 5,280	Minneapolis, Minn., U. S. 815	Whitehorse, Canada. 2,083
Des Moines, Iowa, U. S. 805	Monterrey, Mex. 1,624	Wichita, Kans., U. S. 1,290
Detroit, Mich., U. S. 585	Montreal, Canada. 63	Wiesbaden, Ger. 470
Dresden, Ger. 402	Moscow (Moskva), Sov. Un. 625	Wilmington, Del., U. S. 135
Duluth, Minn., U. S. 610	Mukden, China. 560	Winnipeg, Canada. 773
Durango, Mex. 6,207	München (Munich), Ger. 1,700	Wrocław (Breslau), Poland. 390
Edinburgh, Scotland. 195	Nancy, France. 225	Wuppertal, Ger. 1,100
El Paso, Texas, U. S. 3,695	Nanking, China. 640	Yakutsk, Sov. Un. 210
Fairbanks, Alaska, U. S. 512	New York, N. Y., U. S. 55	Yokohama, Japan. 110
Fès, French Morocco. 1,020	Nice, France. 94	Zacatecas, Mex. 8,010
Flagstaff, Ariz., U. S. 6,890	Nürnberg, Ger. 1,150	Zagreb, Yugoslavia. 430
Florence (Firenze), Italy. 165	Oklahoma City, Okla., U. S. 1,195	Zürich, Switz. 1,360

PRINCIPAL MOUNTAINS OF THE WORLD

NORTH AMERICA

	Height (feet)
McKinley, ^Alaska (^United States; ^North America)	20,320
Logan, ^Canada (^St. Elias Mts.)	19,850
Citlaltepetl (Orizaba), ^Mexico	18,696
St. Elias, Alaska–Canada	18,008
Popocatepetl, Mexico	17,887
Foraker, Alaska	17,395
Ixtacihuatl, Mexico	17,343
Whitney, ^California	14,495
Elbert, ^Colorado (^Rocky Mts.)	14,431
Harvard, Colorado	14,420
Massive, Colorado	14,418
Rainier, ^Washington (^Cascade Range)	14,410
Williamson, California	14,384
Blanca Pk., Colorado (^Sangre de Cristo Range)	14,317
Uncompahgre Pk., Colorado (^San Juan Mts.)	14,301
Grays Pk., Colorado (^Front Range)	14,274
Evans, Colorado	14,260
Longs Pk., Colorado	14,255
Colima, Nevado de, Mexico	14,235
Shasta, California	14,162
Pikes Peak, Colorado	14,110
Tajumulco, ^Guatemala (^Central America)	13,816
Gannett Pk., ^Wyoming	13,785
Grand Teton, Wyoming	13,766
Kings Pk., ^Utah	13,498
Waddington, Canada (^Coast Mts.)	13,260
Cloud Pk., Wyoming (^Big Horn Mts.)	13,175

SOUTH AMERICA

	Height (feet)
Aconcagua, ^Argentina (^Andes Mts.; ^South America)	22,834
Ojos del Salado, Nudos, Argentina–^Chile	22,590
Pissis, Argentina	22,546
Tupungato, Argentina–Chile	22,310
Mercedario, Argentina	22,211
Huascarán, ^Peru	22,205
Llullaillaco, Argentina–Chile	22,146
Yerupaja, Peru	21,758
Incahuasi, Argentina–Chile	21,719
Illampú, Bolivia	21,490
Ancohuma, ^Bolivia	21,489
Sajama, Bolivia	21,391
Illimani, Bolivia	21,151
Chimborazo, ^Ecuador	20,577
Cotopaxi, Ecuador	19,344
Misti, El, Peru	19,144
Cristóbal Colón, ^Colombia	18,947
Huila, Colombia (^Cordillera Central)	18,865
Columna, La, ^Venezuela	16,411
Bandeira, Pico da, ^Brazil	9,462

EUROPE

	Height (feet)
Elbrus, Soviet Union (^Caucasus Mts.; ^Europe)	18,468
Shkhara, Soviet Union	17,059
Dykh-Tau, Soviet Union	17,054
Kazbek, Soviet Union	16,554
Blanc, Mont, ^France (^Alps)	15,781

Wheeler Pk., △New Mexico....13,160
Boundary Pk., △Nevada....13,145
Robson, Canada (△Canadian Rockies)....12,972
Chirripó Grande, △Costa Rica....12,861
Granite Pk., △Montana....12,799
Humphreys Pk., △Arizona....12,670
Borah Pk., △Idaho....12,662
Gunnbjörn, △Greenland....12,139
San Gorgonio, California (△So. Calif.)....11,485
Chiriquí, △Panama....11,410
Hood, △Oregon....11,245
Lassen Pk., △California....10,466
Tina, △Dominican Rep. (△West Indies)....9,285
Paricutín, Mexico....9,100
Selle, Massif de la, △Haiti....8,793
Guadalupe Pk., △Texas....8,751
Olympus, Washington (△Olympic Mts.)....7,954
Santa Ana, △El Salvador....7,828
Blue Mountain Pk., △Jamaica....7,520
Harney Pk., △South Dakota (△Black Hills)....7,242
Mitchell, △North Carolina
 (△Appalachian Mts.)....6,684
Clingman's Dome, North Carolina–
 △Tennessee (△Great Smoky Mts.)....6,642
Turquino, Pico de, △Cuba....6,496
Washington, △New Hampshire (△White Mts.)....6,288
Marcy, △New York (△Adirondack Mts.)....5,344
Katahdin, △Maine....5,268
Pelée, △Martinique....4,800
Mansfield, △Vermont (△Green Mts.)....4,393

Rosa, Monte (Dufourspitze) (△Switzerland)....15,217
Rosa, Monte (Grenzgipfel) (△Italy–Switzerland)....15,194
Weisshorn, Switzerland....14,803
Matterhorn, Switzerland....14,685
Finsteraarhorn, Switzerland....14,026
Jungfrau, Switzerland....13,668
Gross Glockner, △Austria....12,461
Tenerife, Pico de, △Spain (△Canary Is.)....12,180
Mulhacén, △Spain (continental)....11,424
Aneto, Pico de, Spain (△Pyrenees)....11,168
Perdido (Perdu), Spain....11,007
Etna, Italy (△Sicily)....10,868
Zugspitze, △Germany....9,721
Stalin Peak (Musala), △Bulgaria....9,592
Corno, Italy (△Apennines)....9,560
Olympus, △Greece....9,550
Triglav, △Yugoslavia....9,393
Korab, △Albania....9,068
Cinto, France (△Corsica)....8,891
Stalin Pk. (Gerlachovka), △Czechoslovakia
 (△Carpathian Mts.)....8,737
Galdhöppigen, △Norway....8,400
Negoi, △Romania....8,346
Rysy Pk., Czechoslovakia....8,212
Parnassós, Greece....8,061
Idhi (Ida), Greece (△Crete)....8,058
Pico, △Portugal (△Azores Is.)....7,611
Kebnekaise, △Sweden....6,962
Hvannadalshnúkur, △Iceland....6,952
Narodnaya, Soviet Union (△Ural Mts.)....6,184

△Highest mountain in state, country, range or region named.

PRINCIPAL MOUNTAINS OF THE WORLD (*Continued*)

EUROPE (Cont.)

	Height (feet)
Marmora, Punta La, Italy (^Sardinia)	6,017
Hekla, Iceland	4,747
Nevis, Ben, ^Scotland	4,406
Haltia, ^Finland	4,344
Vesuvius, Italy	3,842
Snowdon, ^Wales	3,560
Carrantuohill, ^Ireland	3,414
Kekes, ^Hungary	3,330
Scafell Pike, ^England	3,210

ASIA

	Height (feet)
Everest, ^China (^Tibet) ^Nepal (^Himalaya Mts.; ^Asia; ^World)	29,028
Godwin Austen (K²), ^India (^Kashmir) (^Karakoram Range)	28,250
Kanchenjunga, Nepal–^Sikkim	28,168
Makalu, China (Tibet)–Nepal	27,790
Dhaulagiri, Nepal	26,810
Nanga Parbat, India (Kashmir)	26,660
Annapurna, Nepal	26,504
Gasherbrum, India (Kashmir)	26,470
Gosainthan, (Tibet) China	26,291
Nanda Devi, India	25,643
Rakaposhi, India (Kashmir)	25,551
Kamet, India	25,447
Namcha Barwa, China (Tibet)	25,445
Tirich Mir, ^Pakistan (^Hindu Kush)	25,426
Gurla Mandhata, China (Tibet)	25,355

	Height (feet)
Anai Mudi, ^India (peninsular)	8,841
Angka, Doi, ^Thailand	8,452
Kwanmo, ^Korea	8,336
Pidurutalagala, ^Ceylon	8,281
Mayon, Philippines (Luzon)	8,071
Asahi, Japan (^Hokkaido)	7,513
Tahan, Gunong, ^Malaya	7,186
Olympus (Troodos), ^Cyprus	6,403
Kuju-San, Japan (Kyushu)	5,866
Atzmon, ^Israel	3,962
Krakatoa (Rakata), Indonesia	2,667
Carmel, Israel	1,791

AFRICA

	Height (feet)
Kilmanjaro (Kibo), ^Tanganyika (^Africa)	19,590
Kenya, ^Kenya	17,040
Ruwenzori (Margherita), ^Congo L.–^Uganda	16,821
Bejeda (Ras Dashan), ^Ethopia	15,158
Elgon, Kenya–Uganda	14,178
Toubkal, Djebal, ^Morocco (^Atlas Mts.)	13,661
Cameroon, ^Nigeria	13,354
Thabantshonyana, ^Basutoland (^Southern Africa)	11,425
Emi Koussi, ^Chad (^Tibesti Mts.)	11,204
Neiges, Piton des, ^Reunion	10,069
Tahat, Algeria (^Ahaggar Mts.)	9,852
Maromókotro, Malagasy	9,468
Santa Isabel, ^Fernando Póo	9,350
Cano, ^Cape Verde Is.	9,760

Ulugh Muztagh, China (△Kunlun Mts.)	25,340
Minya Konka, China	24,900
Stalin Pk., △Soviet Union (△Pamir-Alay Mts.)	24,590
Pobeda Pk., China–Soviet Union (△Tien Shan)	24,409
Muztagh Ata, China	24,388
Lenin Pk., Soviet Union	23,382
Tengri Khan, Soviet Union	22,940
Kailas, China (Tibet)	22,028
Demavend, △Iran	18,934
Ararat, △Turkey	16,946
Carstensz, △Neth. New Guinea (△New Guinea)	16,503
Klyuchevskaya, Soviet Union (△Kamchatka)	15,912
Wilhelmina, Neth. New Guinea	15,518
Tabun Bogdo (Khuitun), △Mongolia (△Altai Mts.)	15,266
Belukha, Soviet Union	15,157
Kinabalu, △North Borneo (△Borneo)	13,455
Hsinkao, China (△Formosa)	13,113
Erciyas, Turkey	12,848
Munku-Sardyk, Mongolia–Soviet Union (△Sayan Mts.)	12,821
Kerintji, △Indonesia (△Sumatra)	12,484
Fuji, △Japan (△Honshu)	12,388
Rindjani, Indonesia (△Lombok)	12,225
Mahameru, Indonesia (△Java)	12,060
Rantemario, Indonesia (△Celebes)	11,286
Qurnet, es Sa'uda, △Lebanon	10,131
Sham, Jabalash, △Oman	9,902
Apo, △Philippines (△Mindanao)	9,690
Pulog, Philippines (△Luzon)	9,612
Hermon, Lebanon–△Syria	9,232
Katherina, Gabel, △Egypt–U.A.R.	8,652
São Tomé, Pico de, △Sao Tome	6,640

OCEANIA

Wilhelm, New Guinea Ter.	15,400
Mauna Kea, △Hawaii (△Hawaii I.)	13,796
Mauna Loa, Hawaii	13,680
Bangeta, New Guinea Ter.	13,434
Victoria, △Papua (△Owen Stanley Range)	13,363
Cook, △New Zealand (△South Island)	12,349
Balbi, △Solomon Is. (△Bougainville)	10,170
Haleakala, Hawaii (△Maui)	10,025
Ruapehu, New Zealand (△North Island)	9,175
Mauga Silisili, △Samoa (Western)	8,000
Orohena, △Fr. Oceania (△Tahiti)	7,618
The Father, New Guinea Ter. (△Bismarck Arch.)	7,546
Kosciusko, △Australia (△New South Wales)	7,328
Panié, △New Caledonia	5,348
Ossa, Australia (△Tasmania)	5,305
Bartle Frere, Australia (△Queensland)	5,287
Kawaikini, Hawaii (△Kauai)	5,170
Woodroffe, Australia (△South Australia)	4,970
Victoria, △Fiji (△Viti Levu)	4,341
Kilauea, Hawaii (Hawaii I.)	4,090
Kaala Pk., Hawaii (△Oahu)	4,025
Bruce, Australia (△Western Australia)	4,024

ANTARCTICA

Fridtjof Nansen (△Antarctica)	18,953
Wade	16,146
Markham	15,100
Erebus	14,997

△Highest mountain in state, country, range or region named.

PRINCIPAL RIVERS OF THE WORLD

River	Length (miles)
Nile, Africa	4,132
Amazon, South America	3,900
Mississippi-Missouri-Red Rock, North America	3,860
Yangtze, Asia	3,430
Hwang Ho (Yellow), Asia	2,903
Congo, Africa	2,900
Amur, Asia	2,802
Lena, Asia	2,653
Mackenzie, North America	2,635
Mekong, Asia	2,600
Niger, Africa	2,590
Yenisey, Asia	2,566
Missouri, North America	2,466
Paraná, South America	2,450
Mississippi, North America	2,348
Irtysh, Asia	2,300
Plata-Paraguay, South America	2,300
Volga, Europe	2,293
Ob, Asia	2,260
Madeira, South America	2,060
Indus, Asia	1,980
Purús, South America	1,900
St. Lawrence, North America	1,900
Rio Grande, North America	1,885
Brahmaputra, Asia	1,800
Orinoco, South America	1,800
São Francisco, South America	1,800
Peace, North America	1,195
Orange, Africa	1,155
Tigris, Asia	1,150
Sung Hua, Asia	1,118
Pechora, Europe	1,100
Dvina, Europe	1,093
Tobol, Asia	1,038
Snake, North America	1,025
Uruguay, South America	1,018
Red, North America	1,000
Churchill, North America	1,000
Marañón, South America	1,000
Senegal, Africa	1,000
Ohio, North America	981
Magdalena, South America	950
Roosevelt (River of Doubt), South America	950
Godavari, Asia	930
Hsi, Asia	930
Oka, Europe	920
Canadian, North America	906
Dnestr, Europe	876
Brazos, North America	870
Salado, South America	870
Tennessee-French Broad, North America	862
Fraser, North America	850
Parnaíba, South America	850

River	Length
Yukon, North America	1,800
Danube, Europe	1,770
Darling, Australia	1,750
Salween, Asia	1,730
Euphrates, Asia	1,675
Syr Darya, Asia	1,653
Zambezi, Africa	1,650
Tocantins, South America	1,640
Araguaia, South America	1,630
Amu Darya, Asia	1,628
Kolyma, Asia	1,615
Murray, Australia	1,600
Angara, Asia	1,550
Ganges, Asia	1,550
Pilcomayo, South America	1,550
Ural, Asia	1,522
Vilyuy, Asia	1,513
Arkansas, North America	1,450
Colorado, North America	1,450
Irrawaddy, Asia	1,425
Dnepr, Europe	1,420
Aldan, Asia	1,392
Negro, South America	1,305
Paraguay, South America	1,290
Kama, Europe	1,261
Xingú, South America	1,230
Don, Europe	1,224
Ucayali, South America	1,220
Columbia, North America	1,214
Saskatchewan, North America	1,205
Juruá, South America	1,200
Colorado, North America	840
Rhine, Europe	820
Narbada, Asia	800
Athabaska, North America	765
Donets, Europe	735
Pecos, North America	735
Green, North America	730
Elbe, Europe	720
James, North America	710
Ottawa, North America	696
White, North America	690
Cumberland, North America	687
Gambia, Africa	680
Yellowstone, North America	671
Tennessee, North America	652
Gila, North America	630
Vistula, Europe	630
Loire, Europe	625
Tagus, Europe	625
North Platte, North America	618
Albany, North America	610
Tisza, Europe	607
Back, North America	605
Ouachita, North America	605
Cimarron, North America	600
Sava, Europe	585
Niemen, Europe	582
Branco, South America	580
Meuse, Europe	575
Oder, Europe	565
Rhône, Europe	500

PRINCIPAL ISLANDS AND DESERTS OF THE WORLD

ISLANDS

	Area (sq. mi.)
Greenland, Arctic Region	840,000
New Guinea, Oceania	316,856
Borneo, Indonesia	286,967
Madagascar, Indian Ocean	228,000
Baffin, Canadian Arctic	183,810
Sumatra, Indonesia	182,859
Honshu, Japan	88,930
Great Britain, North Atlantic Ocean	88,756
Ellesmere, Canadian Arctic	82,119
Victoria, Canadian Arctic	81,930
Celebes, Indonesia	72,986
South Island, New Zealand	58,897
Java, Indonesia	50,745
North Island, New Zealand	44,281
Cuba, West Indies	44,217
Newfoundland, North Atlantic Ocean	42,734
Luzon, Philippines	40,814
Iceland, North Atlantic Ocean	39,768
Mindanao, Philippines	36,906
Ireland, North Atlantic Ocean	32,596
Novaya Zemlya, Soviet Arctic	31,390
Hokkaido, Japan	29,950
Hispaniola, West Indies	29,522
Sakhalin, Soviet Union	29,344
Tasmania, Australia	26,215
Ceylon, Indian Ocean	25,332

	Area (sq. mi.)
Cyprus, Mediterranean Sea	3,572
Kodiak, Gulf of Alaska	3,569
Puerto Rico, West Indies	3,435
Corsica, Mediterranean Sea	3,367
Crete, Mediterranean Sea	3,238
Leyte, Philippine	3,090
Guadalcanal, Oceania	2,470
Wrangel, Soviet Arctic	1,806
Long Island, United States	1,620

DESERTS

	Estimated Area* (sq. mi.)
Sahara, Northern Africa	3,000,000
Libyan (part of Sahara Desert), Northeastern Africa	650,000
Australian, West and Central Australia	600,000
Arabian, Arabian Peninsula	500,000
Gobi, Mongolia	400,000
Rub al Khali (part of Arabian Desert), Southeastern Saudi Arabia	250,000
Kalahari, Bechuanaland	200,000
Great Sandy (part of Australian Desert), Northwestern Australia	160,000
Great Victoria (part of Australian Desert), Southwestern Australia	125,000

210

Island	Area (sq mi)
Banks, Canadian Arctic	23,230
Devon, Canadian Arctic	20,861
Tierra del Fuego, Argentina-Chile	18,600
Kyushu, Japan	16,215
Melville, Canadian Arctic	16,141
Southampton, Hudson Bay, Canada	15,700
West Spitsbergen, Arctic Region	15,260
New Britain, Oceania	14,592
Formosa, China Sea	13,885
Hainan, South China Sea	13,127
Timor, Oceania	13,094
Prince of Wales, Canadian Arctic	12,830
Vancouver, Canada	12,408
Sicily, Mediterranean Sea	9,925
Somerset, Canadian Arctic	9,370
Sardinia, Mediterranean Sea	9,301
Shikoku, Japan	7,245
New Caledonia, Oceania	7,202
North East Island, Svalbard Group	6,350
Ceram, Indonesia	6,046
Flores, Indonesia	5,860
Samar, Philippines	5,124
Negros, Philippines	4,903
Palawan, Philippines	4,500
Jamaica, West Indies	4,411
Panay, Philippines	4,448
Hawaii, Oceania	4,030
Cape Breton, Canada	3,973
Bougainville, Oceania	3,880
New Ireland, Oceania	3,800
Mindoro, Philippines	3,794

Desert	Area*
Syrian (part of Arabian Desert), Northern Arabian Peninsula	125,000
Northern Arabian Peninsula	125,000
Taklamakan, Southern Sinkiang, China	120,000
Arunta (part of Australian Desert), Central Australia	120,000
Kara Kum, Southern Turkestan, Soviet Union	105,000
Nubian (part of Sahara Desert), Sudan	100,000
Thar or Indian, Northwestern India	100,000
Kyzyl-Kum, Central Turkestan, Soviet Union	90,000
Gibson (part of Australian Desert), Western Australia	85,000
Atacama, Northern Chile	70,000
Nefud (part of Arabian Desert), North and Central Saudi Arabia	50,000
Dasht-i-Lut, Eastern Iran	20,000
Dasht-i-Kavir, North Central Iran	18,000
Peski Muyun-Kum, Eastern Turkestan, Soviet Union	17,000
Mojave, Southern California	13,500
Sechura, Northwestern Peru	10,000
Vizcaíno, Baja California, Mexico	6,000
Painted, Northeastern Arizona	5,000
Great Salt Lake, Northwestern Utah	4,000
Colorado, Southeastern California	3,000
High, Central Oregon	3,000
Grande, Sonora, Mexico	2,500
Black Rock, Northwestern Nevada	600
Smoke Creek, Northwestern Nevada	300

* Many areas given are based on boundaries not clearly defined

PRINCIPAL WATERFALLS OF THE WORLD

NORTH AMERICA

	Height (Feet)
Yosemite (Upper, Central, and Lower Falls), Yosemite National Park, California	2,425
Ribbon, Yosemite National Park, California	1,612
Upper Yosemite, Yosemite National Park, California	1,430
Takakkaw, British Columbia, Canada	1,200
Silver Strand, Yosemite National Park, California	1,170
Middle Cascade, Yosemite National Park, California	910
Bridal Veil, Yosemite National Park, California	620
Multnomah, Oregon	620
Nevada, Yosemite National Park, California	594
Illilouette, Yosemite National Park, California	370
Comet, Washington	320
Lower Yosemite, Yosemite National Park, California	320
Vernal, Yosemite National Park, California	317
Grand, Labrador	315
Virginia, Northwest Territories, Canada	315
Lower Yellowstone, Wyoming	308
Sluiskin, Washington	300
Snoqualmie, Washington	270
Seven, Colorado	266
Montmorency, Quebec, Canada	265
Taughannock, New York	215
Shoshone, Idaho	210
Palouse, Washington	198
Narada, Washington	168
Niagara, New York	167
Manitou, Wisconsin	160

	Height (Feet)
Victoria, Southern Rhodesia	350
Karkloof, South Africa	340

ASIA

	Height (Feet)
Gersoppa, India	829
Kegon, Japan	350
Cauvery, India	320

SOUTH AMERICA

	Height (Feet)
Angel, Venezuela	3,700
Kukenaam, Venezuela	2,000
Tequendama, Columbia	460
Guayra, Brazil-Paraguay	375
Paulo Affonso, Brazil	270
Iguaçu (Iguassu), Argentina-Brazil	210

EUROPE

	Height (Feet)
Kile, Norway	1,800
Reichenbach, Switzerland	1,800
Gavarnie, France	1,385
Skjaeggedals, Norway	1,300

Tower, Yellowstone National Park, Wyoming... 132
Upper Yellowstone, Wyoming... 109
Upper Mesa, Idaho... 106

OCEANIA

	Height (Feet)
Sutherland, New Zealand	1,904
Wollomombie, Australia	1,700

AFRICA

	Height (Feet)
Tugela, South Africa	2,800
King George VI, British Guiana	1,200
Chirombo, Northern Rhodesia	880
King Edward VIII, British Guiana	840
Kalambo, Northern Rhodesia	786
Kaieteur, British Guiana	741
Maletsunyane, Basutoland	630
Marina, British Guiana	500
Baratieri, Ethiopia	460
King George's (or Aughrabies), South Africa	400
Murchison, Uganda	400
Howick, South Africa	360

Krimml, Austria... 1,250
Giessbach, Switzerland... 1,148
Staubbach, Switzerland... 980
Trümmelbach, Switzerland... 950
Vetti, Norway... 820
Maradals, Norway... 650
Skykje, Norway... 650
Terni, Italy... 590
Tosa, Italy... 540
Vorings, Norway... 535
Glomach, Scotland... 370
Rjukan, Norway... 345
Schleier, Autria... 330
Bären, Austria... 296
Eikedals, Norway... 282
Lower Gastein, Austria... 280
Handeck, Switzerland... 250
Harspränget, Sweden... 250
Pissevache, Switzerland... 230
Pistyll Rhaidr, Wales... 230
Upper Gastein, Austria... 205
Golling, Austria... 200
Kessel, Austria... 196
Pistyll Cain, Wales... 150
Stora Sjöfallet, Sweden... 130
Schaffhausen, Switzerland... 100

PRINCIPAL OCEANS, SEAS AND LAKES OF THE WORLD

OCEANS AND SEAS	Area (sq. mi.)	Average Depth (feet)	Greatest Depth (feet)
Pacific Ocean	63,985,000	14,040	35,800
Atlantic Ocean	31,529,000	12,880	30,246
Indian Ocean	28,357,000	13,000	24,444
Arctic Ocean	5,541,000	4,200	17,500
Mediterranean Sea	1,145,000	4,500	15,564
South China Sea	895,000	5,400	16,456
Bering Sea. N. Pac.	878,000	1,665	13,420
Caribbean Sea	750,000	8,400	23,750
Gulf of Mexico	700,000	4,700	12,426
Okhotsk Sea, Asia	582,000	3,000	12,621
East China Sea	480,000	610	8,920
Yellow Sea, Asia	480,000	160	348
Hudson Bay	472,000	440	846
Japan Sea	405,000	4,835	13,241
North Sea, Europe	221,000	180	2,165
Red Sea, Africa-Asia	178,000	1,490	9,301
Black Sea, Europe-Asia	168,500	4,300	7,362
Baltic Sea, Europe	158,000	221	1,400

LAKES	Area (sq. mi.)
Caspian, Soviet Union-Iran (salt)	152,123
Superior, United States-Canada	31,820
Victoria, Kenya-Uganda-Tanganyika	26,828
Aral, Soviet Union	26,525
Huron, United States-Canada	23,010
Michigan, United States	22,400
Tanganyika, Tanganyika	12,355
Baykal, Soviet Union	12,162
Great Bear, Canada	12,000

LAKES	Area (sq. mi.)
Great Slave, Canada	11,170
Nyasa, Rhodesia & Nyasaland	10,900
Erie, United States-Canada	9,940
Winnipeg, Canada	9,094
Chad, Chad-Niger	8,000
Ontario, United States-Canada	7,540
Ladoga, Soviet Union	7,104
Balkhash, Soviet Union	6,680
Onega, Soviet Union	3,822
Eyre, Australia	3,700
Rudolf, Kenya	3,500
Titicaca, Peru-Bolivia	3,261
Nicaragua, Nicaragua	3,060
Athabaska, Canada	3,058
Reindeer, Canada	2,440
Torrens, Australia	2,400
Koko Nor, China	2,300
Issyk-Kul, Soviet Union	2,200
Vänern, Sweden	2,150
Winnipegosis, Canada	2,086
Bangweulu, Rhodesia & Nyasaland	2,000
Urmia, Iran (salt)	1,900
Manitoba, Canada	1,817
Albert, Uganda-Congo L.	1,750
Great Salt, United States (salt)	1,700
Leopold II, Congo L.	1,700
Dubawnt, Canada	1,650
Nipigon, Canada	1,640
Gairdner, Australia	1,500
Lake of the Woods, United States-Canada	1,500
Van, Turkey	1,450

PRINCIPAL SHIP CANALS AND TUNNELS OF THE WORLD

SHIP CANALS	Year Completed	Length (miles)	Depth (feet)	Width (feet)
Baltic-White Sea, Soviet Union	1933	141	...	...
Suez, Egypt, U.A.R.	1869	103	34	197
Albert, Belgium	1939	82	16	56
Moscow-Volga, Soviet Union	1937	79	20	89
Kiel, Germany	1895	61	45	146
Göta, Sweden	1832	56	10	47
Panama, Canal Zone	1914	51	41	300
Houston, Texas	1925	49	30	195
Beaumont-Port Arthur, Texas	1930	46	32	125
Elbe and Trave, Germany	1900	41	12	72
Manchester, England	1894	35.5	26	85
Chicago Sanitary and Ship, Illinois	1900	28	20	110
Welland, Canada	1932	27.6	25	200
Gent-Terneuzen, Belgium-Netherlands	1929	21	20	76
Princess Juliana, Netherlands	1935	20	16	52
Amsterdam-North Sea, Netherlands	1876	16.5	35	120
Kronshtadt-Leningrad, Soviet Union	1890	16	20.5	220
Chesapeake and Delaware, Maryland-Delaware	1927	14	27	200
Lake Washington, Washington	1916	8.5	29	80
Cape Cod, Massachusetts	1914	8	32	500
New Orleans Industrial, Louisiana	1921	6	30	150
Kórinthos, Greece	1893	4	26.2	72
Keeweenaw, Michigan	1930	2	22	200
Sault Ste. Marie, Michigan	1919	1.6	22	100
Sault Ste. Marie, Canada	1895	1.4	18.3	142

TUNNELS	Length (miles)	Purpose	Year Completed
Simplon, Italy-Switzerland	12.3	Railway	1906
Apennine, Italy	11.0	Railway	1930
Saint Gotthard, Switzerland	9.3	Railway	1882
Lötschberg, Switzerland	9.0	Railway	1912
Mont Cenis, France-Italy	8.0	Railway	1870
Cascade, Washington	7.8	Railway	1929
Vosges, France	7.0	Railway	1937
Arlberg, Austria	6.4	Railway	1884
Moffat, Colorado	6.1	Railway	1927
Tauern, Austria	5.5	Railway	1909
Giovi, Italy	5.4	Railway	1880
Arthur's Pass, New Zealand	5.3	Railway	1924
Connaught, British Columbia, Canada	5.0	Railway	1916
Hoosac, Massachusetts	4.7	Railway	1875
Rove, France	4.5	Ship	1927
Severn, England	4.3	Railway	1887
Col de Braus, France-Italy	3.7	Railway	1928
Viella, Spain	3.1	Vehicular	1948
Mont-Grazian, France-Italy	2.4	Railway	1928
Liverpool-Birkenhead, England	2.1	Vehicular	1934
St. Clair River, Port Huron, Michigan	2.0	Railway	1891
Summit, Argentina-Chile	1.9	Railway	1910
Holland Tunnels, New York City, New York	1.7	Vehicular	1927
Lincoln Tunnels, New York City, New York	1.4	Vehicular	1945
Blackwall, England	1.3	Vehicular	1897
AQUEDUCT TUNNELS			
Delaware, New York	85.3	City water supply	1950
City Tunnel No. 2, New York	20.0	City water supply	1936
City Tunnel No. 1, New York	18.1	City water supply	1926
Alva B. Adams, Colorado	13.1	Water diversion	1946
Tequixquiac, Mexico City, Mexico	6.0	Sewage	1900
Gunnison, Colorado	5.8	Irrigation	1909

PRINCIPAL DAMS

	Height (feet)	Volume* (cu. yds.)	Year Completed
Hoover, Colorado River, Arizona-Nevada.	726	4,400,000	1936
Shasta, Sacramento River, California.....	602	6,541,000	1945
Hungry Horse, South Fork of Flathead River, Montana...................	564	2,900,000	1953
Grand Coulee, Columbia River, Washington......................	550	10,585,000	1942
Ross, Skagit River, Washington.........	545	879,000	1949
Fontana, Little Tennessee River, North Carolina..........................	480	2,812,000	1944
Anderson Ranch, South Fork of Boise River, Idaho......................	456	9,653,300	1955
Chambon, Romanche River, France......	452	....	1934
Detroit, North Santiam River, Oregon....	440	1,670,000	1948
Pine Flat, Kings River, California.......	440	2,240,000	1954
O'Shaughnessy, Tuolumne River, California...........................	430	675,000	1938
Mud Mountain, White River, Washington.	425	2,230,000	1942
Owyhee, Owyhee River, Oregon.........	417	537,200	1932
Diablo, Skagit River, Washington.......	386	350,000	1930
San Gabriel No. 1, San Gabriel River, California...........................	381	10,641,000	1938
Pacoima, Pacoima Creek, California......	372	225,300	1928
Pardee, Mokelumne River, California.....	358	615,000	1929
Arrowrock, Boise River, Idaho...........	350	636,000	1937
Genissiat, Rhône River, France..........	345	875,000	1949
Alder, Nisqually River, Washington......	330	440,000	1944
Morris, San Gabriel River, California.....	328	446,000	1934
Salt Springs, North Fork of Mokelumne River, California....................	328	3,171,500	1931
Exchequer, Merced River, California.....	326	390,600	1926
Buffalo Bill, Shoshone River, Wyoming...	325	82,900	1910
Castillon, Verdon River, France.........	325	....	**
Parker, Colorado River, Arizona– California...........................	320	380,000	1938
Watauga, Watauga River, Tennessee.....	320	3,500,000	1949
Friant, San Joaquin River, California.....	319	2,134,700	1944
Ariel, Lewis River, Washington..........	313	307,000	1931
Green Mountain, Blue River, Colorado...	309	4,406,000	1943
Hiwassee, Hiwassee River, North Carolina.	307	807,200	1940
Kensico, Bronx River, New York........	307	900,000	1916
Lázaro Cárdenas, Nazas River, Mexico...	302	6,931,870	1947
Elephant Butte, Rio Grande River, New Mexico...........................	301	629,400	1916
Horse Mesa, Salt River, Arizona.........	300	162,900	1927
La Angostura, Bavispe River, Mexico....	299	190,237	1942
Granby, Colorado River, Colorado.......	295	2,901,300	1951

216

OF THE WORLD

	Height (feet)	Volume* (cu. yds.)	Year Completed
Seminoe, North Platte River, Wyoming . . .	295	210,200	1939
New Croton, Croton River, New York	294	855,000	1906
San Gabriel No. 2, West Fork of San Gabriel River, Calif.	290	1,200,000	1935
South Holston, South Fork of Holston River, Tennessee.	290	. . . .	1950
Bartlett, Verde River, Arizona.	287	182,300	1939
Don Pedro, Tuolumne River, California . .	284	296,600	1923
Cushman No. 1, North Fork of Skokomish River, Wash.	280	90,000†	1926
Roosevelt, Salt River, Arizona.	280	355,800	1911
Winsor, Swift River, Massachusetts.	280	4,000,000	1939
Morena, Cottonwood Creek, California. . .	279	355,000	1930
Bull Shoals, White River, Arkansas.	278	2,100,000	1952
Marshall Ford, Colorado River, Texas. . . .	278	3,389,000	1942
Dix River, Dix River, Kentucky.	275	1,747,000	1925
Lake Spaulding, South Fork of Yuba River, California.	275	191,800	1919
El Capitan, San Diego River, California. .	270	2,679,700	1935
Folsom, American River, California.	268	14,000,000	1954
Alcova, North Platte River, Wyoming. . . .	265	1,635,300	1938
Norris, Clinch River, Tennessee.	265	1,184,000	1936
Cobble Mountain, Little River Massachusetts.	263	1,799,200	1932
Shannon, Baker River, Washington.	263	132,000	1925
Upper Narrows, Yuba River, California . . .	260	380,000	1941
Lake Pleasant, Agua Fria River, Arizona.	256	98,400	1927
Ashokan, Esopus Creek, New York	252	2,471,900	1912
Big Tijunga, Big Tijunga Creek, California.	251	80,000†	1931
Coolidge, Gila River, Arizona.	250	204,000	1928
Fort Peck, Missouri River, Montana.	250	128,000,000	1940
Look-out Point, Middle Fork of Willamette River, Oregon.	250	10,600,000	1954
Nantahala, Nantahala River, North Carolina.	250	1,829,000	1942
Burrinjuck, Murrumbidgee River, Australia.	247	772,000	1927
Hume, Murray River, Australia.	172	. . . .	1936
Aswan, Nile River, Egypt, U.A.R.	170	. . . .	1930
Denison, Red River, Oklahoma–Texas. . . .	165	15,475,000	1943
Kingsley, North Platte River, Nebraska. .	162	26,000,000	1941
Dnepropetrovsk, Dnepr River, Soviet Union.	145	. . . .	1932
Gatun, Chagres River, Panama Canal Zone.	115	22,958,089	1912

* Total volume of material used in dam.
† Volume of concrete or masonry only.   **Under construction.

PRINCIPAL DISCOVERIES

DATE	EXPLORER	COUNTRY REPRE-SENTED	DESCRIPTION
Ancient and Medieval (to the Discovery of America)			
600 B.C.	Phoenician Sailors	Egypt	Reported by Herodotus to have sailed around Africa from east to west in three years, under orders of King Necho.
500-450 B.C.	Himilco	Carthage	Said to have explored the west coast of Europe, possibly reaching Britain.
500 B.C.	Hanno	Carthage	Explored west coast of Africa to Sierra Leone or about 5°N.
450 B.C.	Herodotus	Greece	Visited Black Sea, eastern Mediterranean, and Egypt, and described the world of his time.
334-323 B.C.	Alexander the Great	Macedonia	Explored and conquered all of southwestern Asia from Egypt to the Jaxartes and Indus rivers.
320 B.C.	Pytheas	Marseilles	Visited Britain and northwestern Europe and, possibly, either Iceland or Norway, which he called Thule.
59-44 B.C.	Julius Caesar	Rome	Added information about Gaul, Britain, and Germany to current geographical knowledge.
20 B.C.	Strabo	Rome	Traveled widely throughout Mediterranean lands; compiled most complete geography of ancient times.
570 A.D.	St. Brendan	Ireland	Alleged to have sailed the western seas for seven years in search of tropical islands; may have reached Madeira or West Indies.
690 A.D.	Bishop Arculf	France	Visited Jerusalem and other holy places; described Egypt.
721-31 A.D.	Willibad	England	Visited and described the Holy Land, Constantinople, and Rome.
890 A.D.	Othere	Norway	Sailed around North Cape, along the Lapland coast, and discovered the White Sea.
925-950 A.D.	Al Masudi	Baghdad	Traveled in India, Ceylon, China, Russia, Persia, and Egypt.
981-86 A.D.	Eric the Red	Norse	Discovered and colonized southern Greenland.
1001 A.D.	Leif Ericsson	Norse	Discovered Labrador, Newfoundland, and nearby coasts.
1003-06 A.D.	Thorfinn Karlsefni	Norse	Explored and attempted to colonize northeast coast of North America.
1099-1154 A.D.	Idrisi	Spain and Sicily	Traveled in north Africa and Asia Minor; compiled a description and map of the world.
1106 A.D.	Daniel of Kiev	Russia	Visited Jaffa, Jerusalem, the Jordan, and Damascus on pilgrimage to the Holy Land.
1160-73 A.D.	Benjamin of Tudela	Spain	Traveled through Egypt, Assyria, Persia, and central Asia, visiting Jewish centers.
1245-47 A.D.	John de Plano Carpini	Italy	Traveled through Poland, Russia, and central Asia to Karakoram, in Mongolia, as legate of the Pope.
1253-55 A.D.	William de Rubruquis	France	Visited Karakoram, in Mongolia, by way of southern Russia and Turkestan.
1270 A.D.	Lancelot Mallocello	Italy	Re-discovered the Fortunate or Canary Islands.
1271-95 A.D.	Marco Polo	Italy	Journeyed to China by way of central Asia; returned by sea by way of Sumatra, Ceylon, India, and Persia; reported existence of Japan and Madagascar.
1281-91 A.D.	Vivaldi Brothers	Italy	Attempted voyage to India by sea along west coast of Africa, but never returned.
1323-28 A.D.	Friar Odoric		Traveled to China by way of India and Malaya; returned through central Asia.
1325-54 A.D.	Ibn Battuta		Visited every Mohammedan country from Spain to India; traveled widely in Far East, Arabia, and western Africa.
1346 A.D.	Jacme Ferrer	Catalonia	Credited by 14th-century maps with having rounded Cape Bojador on west coast of Africa.
1427-31 A.D.	Diogo de Seville	Portugal	Discovered some of the Azores Islands.
1433-35 A.D.	Gil Eannes	Portugal	Rounded Cape Bojador in exploration of west coast of Africa.
1435-36 A.D.	Affonso Baldaya	Portugal	Landed on coast of Africa in vicinity of Rio de Oro.
1441-46 A.D.	Nuno Tristam	Portugal	Reached the Senegal R. along west coast of Africa.
1445 A.D.	Dinis Diaz	Portugal	Rounded Cape Verde on west coast of Africa.
1455-57 A.D.	Alvise da Cadamosto	Portugal	Explored the Senegal and Gambia rivers; discovered Cape Verde Islands.
1472 A.D.	Fernando Po	Portugal	Discovered island bearing his name in Gulf of Guinea.
1482-86 A.D.	Diogo Cao	Portugal	Discovered mouth of Congo R. (1482), reached Cape Negro at 16°S. (1486).

DATE	EXPLORER	COUNTRY REPRE- SENTED	DESCRIPTION
1487 A.D.	Pedro de Covilha	Portugal	Traveled to India via Egypt and Arabia: visited east coast of Africa, south to Zambezi R.
1487-88 A.D.	Bartolomeu Diaz	Portugal	Discovered Cape of Good Hope: explored coast east to Mossell Bay.
America (1492-1850)			
1492- 1502 A.D.	Christopher Columbus	Spain	Discovered the West Indies (1492); in three later voyages explored coasts of northern South America and Central America.
1497-98 A.D.	John and Sebastian Cabot	England	Discovered shores of Nova Scotia and New- foundland, and visited southern Greenland.
1499- 1500 A.D.	Amerigo Vespucci, Juan de la Cosa and Alonso de Ojeda	Spain	Discovered and explored northeastern coast of South America.
1499- 1500 A.D.	Vincente Yanez Pinzón	Spain	Discovered mouth of Amazon R.
1500 A.D.	Pedro Alvares Cabral	Portugal	Discovered or visited coast of Brazil on voyage to India.
1500-01 A.D.	Gaspar Corte Real	Portugal	Made two voyages to northeastern North America, but never returned.
1501-02 A.D.	Amerigo Vespucci	Portugal	Explored coast of Brazil to 30° or farther.
1513 A.D.	Juan Ponce de Leon	Spain	Discovered and explored coasts of Florida.
1513 A.D.	Vasco Nunez de Balboa	Spain	Crossed Isthmus of Panama and discovered the South Sea (Pacific Ocean).
1515 A.D.	Juan Diaz de Solis	Spain	Explored mouth of Rio de la Plata.
1517 A.D.	Francisco Hernandez de Córdova	Spain	Discovered Yucatan and evidence of Mayan culture.
1518 A.D.	Juan de Grijalva	Spain	Explored east coast of Mexico north of Yucatan.
1519 A.D.	Alvárez Pineda	Spain	Explored Gulf of Mexico and may have dis- covered mouth of Mississippi R.
1519-22 A.D.	Ferdinand Magellan	Spain	Discovered Strait of Magellan (1520) during first circumnavigation of the earth.
1519-27 A.D.	Hernando Cortez	Spain	Explored and conquered Mexico.
1523-41 A.D.	Francisco Picarro	Spain	Explored northwestern South America and conquered Peru.
1524 A.D.	Giovanni da Verrazano	France	Discovered New York Bay and explored coast northward.
1524-25 A.D.	Esteban Gomez	Spain	Sailed along east coast of North America from Nova Scotia to Florida.
1527-37 A.D.	Cabeza de Vaca	Spain	Wandered for nine years along and near coast of Gulf of Mexico from Florida to Mexico.
1534-41 A.D.	Jacques Cartier	France	Explored Gulf of St. Lawrence (1534) and river as far as sites of Quebec and Montreal (1536).
1535-36 A.D.	Diego d'Almagro	Spain	Explored and conquered Chile.
1536-38 A.D.	Gonzalo Jiménez de Quesada	Spain	Explored and conquered New Granada, and founded Bogotá.
1539 A.D.	Francisco de Ulloa	Spain	Explored Gulf of California to its head.
1539-43 A.D.	Hernando de Soto	Spain	Explored southeastern United States from Florida to Tennessee; discovered Mississip- pi R. (1541).
1540 A.D.	Hernando de Alarcón	Spain	Sailed up Gulf of California and entered Colorado R.
1540-42 A.D.	Francisco Vasquez de Coronado	Spain	Led expedition into southwestern United States; explored Great Plains northward to Kansas; Grand Canyon of Colorado R. dis- covered by one of his party.
1541 A.D.	Francisco de Orellana	Spain	Crossed the Andes and descended Amazon R. to its mouth.
1542-43 A.D.	Bartolomé Ferrelo and Juan Rod- riguez Cab- rillo	Spain	Discovered San Diego Bay and explored California coast to about 42° N. or Cape Mendocino.
1562-65 A.D.	René de Lau- donnière, and Jean de Ribaut	France	Failed in effort to establish a permanent colony on coast of South Carolina.

DATE	EXPLORER	COUNTRY REPRESENTED	DESCRIPTION
		America (1492-1850)—Continued	
1576-78 A.D.	Martin Frobisher	England	Made three voyages in search of the Northwest Passage; discovered and explored Frobisher Bay.
1577-80 A.D.	Francis Drake	England	Explored west coast of North America to 46° or 48° N. and named it New Albion; circumnavigated the earth.
1583 A.D.	Humphrey Gilbert	England	Made first effort to establish an English colony in North America; ship lost returning to England.
1585-87 A.D.	John Davis	England	Made several voyages in search of Northwest Passage; discovered Davis Strait and Baffin Bay.
1602-03 A.D.	Sebastian Vizcaino and Martin Aguilar	Spain	Sailed along coast of California to about 42° or 43° N.; discovered Monterey Bay but missed that of San Francisco; Aguilar reported large river near 43° N.
1603-15 A.D.	Samuel de Champlain	France	Explored and mapped St. Lawrence R., New England coast, Ottawa R., Lake Huron, Lake Ontario; discovered Lake Champlain (1609).
1607-14 A.D.	John Smith	England	Explored and mapped vicinity of Jamestown, Virginia, (1608) and coast of New England (1614).
1609-11 A.D.	Henry Hudson	Holland and England	Explored Hudson R. to Albany for Holland (1609); discovered and explored Hudson Bay for England (1610-1611).
1612-13 A.D.	Thomas Button	England	Explored Hudson Bay in search of strait to the Western Ocean.
1615-16 A.D.	William Baffin	Engalnd	Made two voyages in search of Northwest Passage; explored Baffin Bay to 78° N.
1631-32 A.D.	Luke Foxe and William James	England	Explored northern and southern extensions of Hudson Bay without finding passage westwards.
1634 A.D.	Jean Nicolet	France	Crossed Lake Huron to Mackinac Strait and Green Bay; reported "Western Sea" three days distant.
1658-59 A.D.	Pierre Radisson and Sieur des Groseillers	France	Explored upper Mississippi R. and western shores of Lake Superior.
1669-70 A.D.	John Lederer	England	Crossed the Blue Ridge and explored the Shenandoah Valley.
1669-87 A.D.	Robert Cavelier de La Salle	France	Explored Lake Ontario and upper Ohio R. (1669) and the Great Lakes to head of Lake Michigan (1679); descended Illinois and Mississippi rivers to Gulf of Mexico (1681-82); killed in Texas after failing to locate Mississippi R. by sea (1684-87).
1673 A.D.	Jacques Marquette and Louis Joliet	France	Descended Mississippi R. from the Wisconsin R. to the Arkansas and returned to the Great Lakes via the Illinois-Chicago portage.
1680 A.D.	Louis Hennepin	France	Explored upper Mississippi R. from the Illinois R. to the Minnesota.
1688 A.D.	Louis de la Hontan	France	Explored upper Mississippi region; spread reports of fictitious "Long River" leading to Western Sea.
1699 A.D.	Pierre le Moyne Iberville	France	Entered mouth of Mississippi from Gulf of Mexico and explored delta.
1701-02 A.D.	Eusebio Francisco Kino	Spain	Explored the Gila and lower Colorado rivers; proved that California was not an island.
1718-19 A.D.	Bernard de la Harpe	France	Explored the Red and Arkansas rivers.
1721 A.D.	Pierre Francois Xavier de Charlevoix	France	Visited French settlements in North America from Quebec to New Orleans.
1728-41 A.D.	Vitus Bering	Russia	Confirmed existence of strait between Asia and America (1728); discovered Northwest coast and named Mt. St. Elias (1741).
1730-43 A.D.	Sieur de La Verendrye and Sons	France	Explored territory northwest of Lake Superior; discovered Lake Winnipeg; sons may have seen Rocky Mountains.
1742 A.D	Christopher Middleton	England	Discovered Repulse Bay in search of passage to Western Sea.
1749 A.D.	Celoron de Bienville	France	Buried plates along the Ohio R., claiming formal possession for France.
1750 A.D.	Thomas Walker	England	Discovered Cumberland Gap route into Kentucky.

DATE	EXPLORER	COUNTRY REPRESENTED	DESCRIPTION
		America (1492-1850)—Continued	
1750 A.D.	Christopher Gist	England	Explored Ohio R. and Kentucky areas.
1766-68 A.D.	Jonathan Carver	England	Explored the upper Mississippi region and reported existence of the Oregon or River of the West.
1769-75 A.D.	Daniel Boone	England	Explored eastern Kentucky (1769-71); and blazed the famous Wilderness Road (1775).
1769 A.D.	Jose Ortega	Spain	Discovered San Francisco Bay during overland expedition into upper California.
1770-71 A.D.	Samuel Hearne	England	Traced the Coppermine R. to the Northern Ocean and discovered Great Slave Lake.
1774-75 A.D.	Juan Perez and Bruno Heceta	Spain	Sent to explore northwest coast, reaching 55° N.; Heceta observed entrance to Columbia R.; Perez discovered Nootka Sound.
1778-79 A.D.	James Cook	England	Re-discovered Hawaiian Islands; explored and charted northwest coast from 45° N. to Arctic Ocean.
1788-92 A.D.	Robert Gray	United States	Explored northwest coast; discovered Grays Harbor; entered and named the Columbia R. (1792).
1789-93 A.D.	Alexander McKenzie	England	Traced McKenzie R. to its mouth (1789); crossed Rocky Mountains via Peace R. and reached Pacific Ocean.
1792-94 A.D.	George Vancouver	England	Explored and mapped Puget Sound; charted inside passage and inlets along northwest coast.
1804-06 A.D.	Meriwether Lewis and Wm. Clark	United States	Ascended Missouri R. to its source, crossed Rocky Mountains and descended Columbia R. to Pacific Ocean.
1805-07 A.D.	Zebulon M. Pike	United States	Explored and mapped upper Mississippi R. (1805); and southwestern section of Louisiana Territory (1806-07).
1807-08 A.D.	Manuel Lisa and John Colter	United States	Explored Northern Rockies (Yellowstone-Big Horn region) as trappers and fur traders.
1811-12 A.D.	Wilson Price Hunt (Astorians)	United States	Discovered overland route to Pacific via the Snake and Columbia rivers
1819-20 A.D.	Stephen H. Long	United States	Explored the high plains between Platte and Arkansas rivers; originated myth of "Great American Desert."
1821 A.D.	William Becknell	United States	Opened trade route between Missouri R. and Santa Fe.
1823-29 A.D.	Jedediah Smith	United States	Located famous South Pass across Rocky Mts.; crossed desert between Colorado R. and California.
1824-28 A.D.	Peter Skene Ogden	England	Explored upper Snake R. and northern Great Basin; discovered Humboldt R. and Great Salt Lake.
1829-30 A.D.	Ewing Young and party	United States	Opened up Spanish Trail between Santa Fe and Los Angeles.
1832-33 A.D.	Nathaniel J. Wyeth	United States	Led first expedition along Oregon Trail to Columbia R.
1833 A.D.	Joseph E. Walker	United States	Crossed Great Basin between Great Salt Lake and California.
1841 A.D.	Charles Wilkes	United States	Visited Oregon country and California during official Pacific exploring expedition by sea.
1842-45 A.D.	John C. Fremont	United States	First official government explorer to retrace explorations of fur trappers in the Far West.
		Africa	
1520-27 A.D.	Francisco Alvarez	Portugal	Visited Ethiopia and described it in detail.
1541 A.D.	Christopher da Gama	Portugal	Led expedition into Ethiopia.
1578-89 A.D.	Duarte Lopez	Portugal	Visited the Kingdom of Congo; his reports a chief source of information until 19th century.
1604-22 A.D.	Pedro Paez	Portugal	First European to visit Ethiopian sources of the Niles R.
1616 A.D.	Gaspar Baccaro	Portugal	Explored interior from upper Zambezi to west coast.
1618-19 A.D.	George Thompson	England	Explored the Gambia R.
1625-35 A.D.	Jerome Lobo	Portugal	Lived in Ethiopia as a missionary.
1698-1700 A.D.	C. J. Poncet	France	Traveled as a physician into Ethiopia to treat the Emperor.

DATE	EXPLORER	COUNTRY REPRESENTED	DESCRIPTION
		Africa—Continued	
1768-73 A.D.	James Bruce	England	Explored Ethiopia, especially source of the Blue Nile R.
1777-79 A.D.	William Patterson	England	Made several trips into the Kaffir country as a naturalist.
1795-1805 A.D.	Mungo Park	England	Explored the Gambia R. and was first modern European to reach the Niger R.
1797-98 A.D.	John Barrow	England	Journeyed from Cape of Good Hope to Upper Orange R.
1797-1800 A.D.	Frederick Hornemann	England	Traveled from Egypt to Murzuk and the Niger R., disguised as an Arab.
1798-99 A.D.	Francisco de Lacerda	Portugal	Explored southeastern interior north of Zambezi R.
1801 A.D.	John Trutter and William Somerville	England	Explored Bechuanaland, north of Orange R.
1802-06 A.D.	Pedro Baptista and A. Jose	Portugal	Made first recorded crossing of continent eastward from Angola.
1812-14 A.D.	J. L. Burckhardt	Switzerland	Traveled up the Nile R. and across the Red Sea.
1822-25 A.D.	ixon Denham and Hugh Clapperton	England	Crossed desert from Tripoli to Lake Chad and westward to the Niger R.
1825-26 A.D.	Alexander G. Laing	England	Reached Timbuktu from Tripoli, but was murdered on return trip.
1827-28 A.D.	Rene Caille	France	Traveled from Guinea Coast to Fez and Tangier by way of Timbuktu.
1830-34 A.D.	Richard Lander	England	Explored the lower Niger R. and located its mouth.
1849-73 A.D.	David Livingstone	England	Discovered Zambezi R. (1851), Victoria Falls (1855), and Lake Nyasa (1859); explored upper Congo tributaries; found by Stanley on Lake Tanganyika in 1871.
1856-59 A.D.	Richard Burton	England	Discovered Lake Tanganyika and explored surrounding area.
1858-63 A.D.	John Speke	England	Discovered Victoria Nyanza as source of the Nile R.
1861-69 A.D.	Samuel Baker	England	Explored upper Nile R.; discovered Lake Albert.
1863-71 A.D.	G. A. Schweinfurth	Germany	Explored extensively in the Sudan and equatorial Africa.
1871-90 A.D.	Henry Stanley	United States	Continued Livingstone's explorations in the lakes region; descended Congo R. to Atlantic Ocean (1877); discovered Stanley Pool and Lake Edward.
1877-86 A.D.	Serpa Pinto	Portugal	Crossed the continent from Angola to Mozambique.
1879-90 A.D.	Joseph Thomson	England	Explored new areas in Tanganyika, Kenya, and Uganda.
1888 A.D.	Samuel Teleki	Hungary	Discovered lakes Rudolph and Stephanie.
		Asia	
1497-99 A.D.	Vasco da Gama	Portugal	Discovered sea route to India by way of South Africa and Indian Ocean.
1502-07 A.D.	Ludovici di Varthema	Portugal	Traveled as convert to Islam in Arabia, Persia, India, and East Indies.
1511 A.D.	Mathias Albuquerque	Portugal	Conquered Malacca, East Indian spice center.
1520-21 A.D.	Thomé Pires	Portugal	Sent to Peking as commercial envoy.
1537-58 A.D.	Fernao Mendes Pinto	Portugal	Described travels in India, China, and Japan.
1549-51 A.D.	Francis Xavier	Portugal	Intoduced Christianity into Japan.
1561-63 A.D.	Anthony Jenkinson	England	Visited Persia by overland route from Russia.
1578-1610 A.D.	Matteo Ricci	Portugal	Established first Christian missions in China.
1603-05 A.D.	Benedict de Goez	Portugal	Made first overland trip to China after Marco Polo.
1603-08 A.D.	John Mildenhall	England	Visited India for East India Company.
1632-68 A.D.	Jean B. Tavernier	France	Traveled as commercial trader in Persia, India, and East Indies.
1656 A.D.	Pieter van Goyer and Jacob von Keyser	Holland	Visited Peking by overland route from Canton.
1665-77 A.D.	John Chardin	France	Described extensive travels in Persia and India.
1683-93 A.D.	Engelbert Kaempfer	Holland	As physician with Dutch embassy, visited and described Siam and Japan.
1715-47 A.D.	John Bell	Russia	Traveled as physician with Russian embassies to Persia and through Siberia to China.

AND EXPLORATIONS—*Continued*

DATE	EXPLORER	COUNTRY REPRE- SENTED	DESCRIPTION
Asia—Continued			
1716-21 A.D.	Ipolito Desideri	Italy	Reached Tibetan city of Lhasa from Kashmir.
1761-64 A.D.	Carsten Niebuhr	Denmark	Explored Yemen, reaching cities of Sana and Mocha; also visited Oman, Syria, and Palestine.
1795-97 A.D.	W. R. Broughton	England	Explored coasts of Hokkaido and Korea.
1839-46 A.D.	Evariste Regis Huc	France	Traveled through interior of China, Mongolia and Tibet.
1851-54 A.D.	M. C. Perry	United States	Opened Japan to foreign trade.
1862-67 A.D.	Peter Kropotkin	Russia	Made geographical surveys of North Manchuria.
1867-88 A.D.	Nikolai Prjevalsky	Russia	Led expeditions into Central Asia, Mongolia, and Tibet; re-discovered Lop-nor.
1868-72 A.D.	Ferdinand Richthofen	Germany	Explored and described most of Chinese Empire.
1869-70 A.D.	J. Halévy	France	Explored interior of southwestern Arabia.
1873 A.D.	Jean Dupuis	France	Explored Tonkin route into China.
1885- 1908 A.D.	Sven Hedin	Sweden	Traveled extensively in Persia, Turkestan, China, and Tibet.
1886- 1904 A.D.	Francis Younghusband	England	Explored and surveyed in Kashmir, Central Asia, and Tibet.
1889-92 A.D.	W. W. Rockhill	United States	Explored eastern Tibet.
1899- 1914 A.D.	Gertrude Bell	England	Traveled widely in Palestine, Mesopotamia and inner Arabia.
1899- 1926 A.D.	Aurel Stein	England	Made archaeological explorations in India, Persia, and central Asia.
1901-06 A.D.	Ellsworth Huntington	United States	Explored upper Euphrates R. and Chinese Turkestan.
1914-29 A.D.	Roy Chapman Andrews	United States	Explored western China and Mongolia as a naturalist, discovering many animal fossils.
1917-32 A.D.	H. St. John Philby	England	Crossed Arabia from sea to sea; explored oases of Nejd.
Arctic Regions			
1553-54 A.D.	Hugh Willoughby and Richard Chancellor	England	Attempted exploration of Northeast Passage; Willoughby lost, but Chancellor reached Archangel and opened trade with Russia.
1576-78 A.D.	Martin Frobisher	England	Made three voyages in search of Northwest Passage; discovered Frobisher Bay.
1585-87 A.D.	John Davis	England	Reached latitude 73° N. in Baffin Bay, exploring Northwest Passage.
1594-97 A.D.	Willem Barents	Holland	Discovered Spitzbergen and reached Novaya Zemlya along Northeast Passage.
1607-11 A.D.	Henry Hudson	England and Holland	Made several voyages in search of both Northeast and Northwest Passages to India; reached 82° N. on east Greenland coast.
1615-16 A.D.	William Baffin and Robert Bylot	England	Explored Baffin Bay; reached 78° N.
1648 A.D.	Simon Dezhnev	Russia	Explored northeastern Siberian coast from the Kolyma to Anadyr rivers.
1728 A.D.	Vitus Bering	Russia	Discovered Bering Strait and the St. Lawrence and Diomede Islands.
1737-42 A.D.	Dimitri Laptiev	Russia	Explored north Siberian coast from Lena R. to Cape Baranov.
1742 A.D.	S. Chelyuskin	Russia	Discovered northernmost point of Asia by land.
1770-73 A.D.	Leakhov	Russia	Discovered the New Siberian Islands.
1773 A.D.	C. J. Phipps	England	Reached 80° 48′ north of Spitzbergen.
1818-27 A.D.	W. E. Parry	England	Explored Canadian arctic and Spitzbergen areas; reached 82° 45′ (1827).
1820-22 A.D.	William Scoresby	England	Discovered Scoresby Sound in eastern Greenland; published standard description of arctic regions.
1825-28 A.D.	F. W. Beechey	England	Explored arctic coast of North America from Bering Strait to Point Barrow.
1829-49 A.D.	John and James Ross	England	Discovered Boothia Peninsula and Gulf; James located North Magnetic Pole (1831); both participated in search for Franklin (1848-49).
1845-48 A.D.	John Franklin	England	Lost two ships and 129 men in attempt to sail through Northwest Passage; reached King William Island.
1850-54 A.D	Richard Collinson and Robert McClure	England	Reached Melville Sound from Bering Strait and proved existence of northwest waterway passage.

DATE	EXPLORER	COUNTRY REPRE-SENTED	DESCRIPTION
		Arctic Regions—Continued	
1853-55 A.D.	E. K. Kane	United States	Explored Smith Sound and Kane Basin; reached 80° 10′ N.
1857-58 A.D.	F. L. McClintock	England	Discovered McClintock, Channel and relics of Franklin expedition on King William Island.
1860-71 A.D.	Charles F. Hall	United States	On third expedition, explored northern shores of Ellesmere Island and Greenland, reaching 82° 26′N.
1871-74 A.D.	Julius Payer and Carl Weyprecht	Austria	Discovered Franz Joseph Land Archipelago.
1876 A.D.	Albert H. Markham	England	Reached 83° 20′ on northwest coast of Greenland.
1878-79 A.D.	N. A. E. Nordenskjöld	Sweden	Completed the Northeast Passage in two seasons in ship *Vega.*
1879-81 A.D.	G. W. DeLong	United States	Explored Arctic Ocean northwest of Bering Strait; ship *Jeannette* and most of party lost.
1881-83 A.D.	A. W. Greely	United States	Explored northern Greenland and Ellesmere Island; party established new record of 83° 24′ N.
1888-96 A.D.	Fridtjof Nansen	Norway	Made first crossing of Greenland (1888); reached record of 86° 14′ during drift of ship *Fram* (1895).
1896-97 A.D.	S. A. Andrée	Sweden	Attempted balloon flight to North Pole from Spitzbergen; remains of party found in 1930 on White Island.
1898-1902 A.D.	Otto Sverdrup	Norway	Explored northern Ellesmere Island and discovered Axel Heiberg Island.
1900-09 A.D.	Robert E. Peary	United States	Made repeated efforts to reach North Pole, succeeding (April 6, 1909) by sledge from Grant Land.
1903-06 A.D.	Roald Amundsen	Norway	Completed first trip through Northwest Passage from east to west.
1907-08 A.D.	F. A. Cook	United States	Claimed to have reached North Pole on April 20, 1908.
1925-26 A.D.	Lincoln Ellsworth	United States	Made flight with Amundsen from Spitzbergen to 87° 43′N. and return; co-leader of dirigible flight over North Pole (1926).
1926 A.D.	Richard Byrd and Floyd Bennett	United States	Made successful flight from Spitzbergen to North Pole and return.
1926-28 A.D.	Umberto Nobile	Italy	Made numerous dirigible flights across arctic region; rescued after *Italia* crashed on ice in 1928.
1937-38 A.D.	Otto Schmidt	Russia	Spent nine months with scientific expedition near North Pole.
		Antarctic Regions	
1738-39 A.D.	Pierre Bovet	France	Discovered Bovet Island south of Africa in latitude 54° S.
1768-75 A.D.	James Cook	England	Established non-existence of southern continent in habitable latitudes; reached record of 71° 10′ S.
1771-73 A.D.	Y. J. Kerguelen	France	Discovered and explored Kerguelen Island in latitude 49° 50′ S., longitude 69° 30′ E.
1819-21 A.D.	Fabian von Bellingshausen	Russia	Circumnavigated Antarctica; discovered Alexander I Land.
1821 A.D.	Nathaniel Palmer	United States	Discovered Palmer Land on sealing expedition.
1823 A.D.	James Weddell	England	Discovered Weddell Sea; reached 74° 15′ S.
1830-32 A.D.	John Biscoe	England	Discovered Biscoe Islands; sighted Enderby Land.
1837-40 A.D.	J. Dumont d'Urville	France	Discovered Adelie Land south of Tasmania.
1840-43 A.D.	James Ross	England	Charted coast in neighborhood of Ross Sea; reached record of 79° 9′ S.
1898-1900 A.D.	Carstens Borchgrevink	Norway and England	Spent winter on continent; reached record of 78° 45′ S.
1902-04 A.D.	Robert F. Scott	England	Explored coast of Edward VII Land; reached 82° 17′ S.
1903-05 A.D.	Jean B. Charcot	France	Explored Palmer Land; discovered Loubet Island.
1908-09 A.D.	Ernest Shackleton	England	Explored head of Ross Sea; reached 88° 23′ S.
1910-12 A.D.	Roald Amundsen	Norway	Discovered Queen Maud Range; reached South Pole Dec. 16, 1911.
1910-12 A.D.	Robert Scott	England	Reached South Pole January 18, 1912; entire party perished during return.
1911-13 A.D.	Douglas	England	Explored coast from King George V Land to

DATE	EXPLORER	COUNTRY REPRE-SENTED	DESCRIPTION
\-	\-	**Antarctic Regions—Continued**	\-
1929-31 A.D.	Mawson		Enderby Land in two expeditions.
1914-17 A.D.	Ernest Shackleton	England	Discovered Caird coast; ship lost in Weddell Sea, but party rescued after many hardships.
1928-30 A.D.	Hubert Wilkins	England	Made first explorations by air.
1928-47 A.D.	Richard Byrd	United States	Established base at Little America and made first flight over South Pole (1929); second expediton remained through winter of 1934; third expedition (1939–40) made extensive aerial explorations; fourth expedition concentrated on scientific work.
1935-36 A.D.	Lincoln Ellsworth	United States	Explored by air between Palmer Peninsula and Little America.
1947-48 A.D.	Finn Ronne	United States	Explored Palmer Peninsula and Weddell Sea by land and air.
\-	\-	**Pacific Ocean and Australia**	\-
1520-21 A.D.	Ferdinand Magellan	Spain	Crossed the Pacific from South America to the Philippines during first circumnavigation of the earth.
1542 A.D.	Lopez de Villalobos	Spain	Sailed from Mexico to the Philippines; discovered Caroline and Palau Islands.
1565 A.D.	Andres de Urdaneta	Spain	Discovered northern sailing route from Philippines to Mexico in latitude of the forties.
1567-95 A.D.	Alvaro de Mendana	Spain	Discovered Solomon, Marshall, and Ellice Islands (1567); also Marquesas and Santa Cruz (1595).
1578 A.D.	Francis Drake	England	Crossed the Pacific from California to the East Indies on first English circumnavigation.
1606 A.D.	Pedro de Quiros	Spain	Discovered Tahiti and New Hebrides Islands.
1616 A.D.	Dirk Hartog	Holland	Explored section of west coast of Australia.
1616 A.D.	William Van Schouten and Jacob Lemaire	Holland	Rounded Cape Horn and crossed Pacific; discovered Bismark Archipelago.
1642-44 A.D.	Abel Tasman	Holland	Discovered Tasmania and part of New Zealand.
1699 A.D.	William Dampier	England	Explored west and northwest coasts of Australia.
1721 A.D.	Jacob Roggeveen	Holland	Discovered Easter Island and Samoa.
1767-69 A.D.	Louis de Bougainville	France	Explored South Pacific islands, including Tahiti, Samoa, and the New Hebrides.
1768-79 A.D.	James Cook	England	Made three voyages into the Pacific; explored coasts of New Zealand and eastern Australia (1769–70); proved non-existence of continental land north of Antarctic Circle (1772–75); discovered Hawaiian Islands and explored northwest coast of North America (1776–79).
1785-88 A.D.	Jean de La Pérouse	France	Explored North Pacific Ocean, especially coasts of Siberia and Japan; lost at sea.
1798 A.D.	George Bass	England	Discovered strait separating Tasmania from Australia.
1802-03 A.D.	Matthew Flinders	England	Explored south coast of Australia and sailed completely around the continent.
1816-22 A.D.	John Oxley	England	Explored the interior of New South Wales, Australia.
1824-25 A.D.	Hamilton Hume and William Hovell	England	Explored interior of southeastern Australia.
1828-45 A.D.	Charles Sturt	England	Discovered the Darling R.; descended Murray R. to its mouth; reached center of continent (1845).
1833-35 A.D.	Charles Darwin	England	Explored South Pacific islands as a naturalist.
1840-41 A.D.	Edward Eyre	England	Crossed southern Australia from Spencer Gulf to King George Sound.
1844-48 A.D.	Ludwig Leichhardt	Germany	Explored interior of northern Queensland and Arnhem Land.
1861 A.D.	Robert Burke and W. J. Wills	England	Succeeded in crossing Australia from Melbourne to Gulf of Carpentaria.
1873 A.D.	Colonel Warburton	England	Crossed western Australia from Alice Springs to the coast, using camels.
1874 A.D.	John Forrest	England	Crossed desert region of Australia from Perth to Adelaide.
1875-76 A.D.	Ernest Giles	England	Made trip across desert from Port Augusta to Perth and return.

225

AIR DISTANCES

	Berlin	Buenos Aires	Calcutta	Capetown	Chicago	Hong Kong	London	Mexico City
Berlin, Germany		7376	4376	5977	4402	5500	574	6037
Buenos Aires, Argentina	7376		10242	4270	5596	11463	6918	4633
Calcutta, India	4376	10242		6026	7981	1534	4954	9495
Capetown, Un. of S. Africa	5977	4270	6026		8449	7372	6005	8511
Chicago, U.S.A.	4402	5596	7981	8449		7790	3950	1673
Hong Kong, Asia	5500	11463	1534	7373	7790		5981	8776
London, England	574	6918	4954	6005	3950	5981		5541
Mexico City, Mexico	6037	4633	9495	8511	1673	8776	5541	
Moscow, Soviet Union	996	8375	3447	6294	4984	4439	1549	6688
New York, U.S.A.	3961	5297	7921	7801	713	8051	3459	2085
Nome, Alaska	4342	8848	5271	10107	3314	4547	4381	4309
Oslo, Norway	515	7613	4459	6494	4040	5337	714	5706
Paris, France	542	6877	4889	5841	4133	5956	213	5706
Peiping (Peking), China	4567	11974	2024	8045	6592	1226	5054	7733
Rio de Janeiro, Brazil	6144	1218	9376	3769	5296	10995	5772	4770
Rome, Italy	734	6929	4496	5249	4808	5768	887	6353
San Francisco, U.S.A.	5657	6474	7809	10241	1858	6894	5355	1885
Singapore, Singapore	6166	9864	1791	6016	9365	1652	6744	10307
Tokyo, Japan	5538	11400	3186	9071	6303	1796	5938	7035
Washington, D.C., U.S.A.	4167	5216	8088	7894	591	8148	3665	1878

STEAMSHIP DISTANCES

	Bombay	Buenos Aires	Capetown	Gibraltar	Hamburg	Honolulu	Le Havre	Lisbon
Bombay, India		9601	5469	5639	7552	9631	7024	6036
Buenos Aires, Argentina	9601		4345	6074	7622	8744	7074	6148
Capetown, Un. of S. Africa	5469	4345		5982	7388	11948	6861	5912
Gibraltar, Gibraltar	5639	6074	5982		1863	10433	1336	350
Hamburg, Germany	7552	7622	7388	1863		11283	573	1543
Honolulu, Hawaii	9631	8744	11948	10433	11283		10757	10363
Le Havre, France	7024	7074	6861	1336	573	10757		1017
Lisbon, Portugal	6036	6148	5912	350	1543	10363	1017	
Liverpool, England	7156	7178	7001	1490	1083	10682	578	1148
Melbourne, Australia	6365	8477	6998	11257	13066	5691	12540	11551
New Orleans, U.S.A.	10927	7233	9382	5271	5935	7046	5315	5377
New York, U.S.A.	9413	6761	7814	3714	4166	7718	3640	3403
Panama Roads, Canal Zone	14921	6311	7417	5038	5888	5395	5363	4968
Port Said, Egypt	3511	8259	6148	2217	4058	12604	3521	2532
Rio de Janeiro, Brazil	8998	1325	3769	4816	6354	9875	5820	4858
San Francisco, U.S.A.	11247	10062	11154	8775	9625		9095	8737
Shanghai, China	5328	13087	8787	10553	12349	4986	11822	10833
Singapore, Singapore	2824	10782	6511	8008	9838	6772	9312	8323
Wellington, New Zealand	7961	6956	7531	12847	13758	4736	12801	12459
Yokohama, Japan	6155	13921	9614	11353	14734	3908	12649	11660

AND STEAMSHIP DISTANCES

Moscow	New York	Nome	Oslo	Paris	Peiping (Peking)	Rio de Janeiro	Rome	San Francisco	Singapore	Tokyo	Washington, D.C.
996	3961	4342	515	542	4567	6114	734	5657	6166	5538	4167
8375	5297	8848	7613	6877	11974	1218	6929	6474	9864	11400	5216
3447	7921	5271	4459	4889	2024	9376	4496	7809	1791	3186	8088
6294	7801	10107	6494	5841	8045	3769	5249	10241	6016	9071	7894
4984	713	3314	4040	4133	6592	5296	4808	1858	9365	6303	591
4439	8051	4547	5337	5956	1226	10995	5768	6894	1652	1796	8148
1549	3459	4381	714	213	5054	5772	887	5355	6744	5938	3665
6688	2085	4309	5706	5706	7733	4770	6353	1885	10307	7035	1878
	4662	4036	1016	1541	3597	7179	1474	5868	5238	4650	4883
4662		3769	3672	3622	6823	4820	4273	2571	9630	6735	205
4036	3769		3836	4574	3428	8586	5082	2547	6148	2983	3792
1016	3672	3836		832	4360	6482	1243	5181	6246	5221	3870
1541	3622	4574	832		5101	5703	682	5441	6671	6033	3828
3597	6823	3428	4360	5101		10768	5047	5902	2774	1307	6922
7179	4820	8586	6482	5703	10768		5684	6619	9774	11535	4797
1474	4273	5082	1243	682	5047	5684		6240	6232	6124	4435
5868	2571	2547	5181	5441	5902	6619	6240		8479	5131	2442
5238	9630	6148	6246	6671	2774	9774	6232	8479		3304	9834
4650	6735	2983	5221	6033	1307	11535	6124	5131	3304		6769
4883	205	3792	3870	3828	6922	4797	4435	2442	9834	6769	

Liverpool	Melbourne	New Orleans	New York	Panama Roads	Port Said	Rio de Janeiro	San Francisco	Shanghai	Singapore	Wellington	Yokohama
7156	6365	10927	9413	14921	3511	8998	11247	5328	2824	7961	6155
7178	8477	7233	6761	6311	8259	1325	10062	13087	10782	6956	13921
7001	6998	9382	7814	7417	6148	3769	11154	8787	6511	7531	9614
1490	11257	5271	3714	5038	2217	4816	8775	10553	8008	12847	11353
1083	13066	5935	4166	5888	4058	6354	9625	12349	9838	13758	14734
10682	5691	7046	7718	5395	12604	9875	2408	4986	6772	4736	3908
578	12540	5315	3640	5363	3521	5820	9095	11822	9312	12801	12649
1148	11551	5377	3403	4968	2532	4858	8737	10833	8323	12459	11660
	12764	5266	3539	5287	3652	5932	9024	12201	9490	12778	13399
12764		10780	11452	9130	9040	9416	8011	6012	4396	1737	5606
5266	10780		1970	1650	7498	5965	5287	11495	13207	9133	10489
3539	11452	1970		2323	5895	5493	6059	12176	11693	9814	11169
5287	9130	1650	2323		7217	5058	3737	9853	12097	7491	8846
3652	9040	7498	5895	7217		7006	10986	8301	5791	10630	9128
5932	9416	5965	5493	5058	7006		8794	12490	10179	7915	13317
9024	8011	5287	6059	3737	10986	8794		6339	8467	6800	5223
12201	6012	11495	12176	9853	8301	12490	6339		2545	6184	1199
9490	4396	13207	11693	12097	5791	10179	8467	2545		5992	3345
12778	1737	9133	9814	7491	10630	7915	6800	6184	5992		5736
13399	5606	10489	11169	8846	9128	13317	5223	1199	3345	5736	

ECONOMIC FACTS FOR PRINCIPAL COUNTRIES

Country	Mineral Resources	Principal Agricultural Products	Principal Manufactures	Principal Occupations % of Total employed
ALGERIA	Iron ore, phosphate, coal, iron pyrites, barite, fuller's earth, zinc ore, lead ore, mercury.	Wheat, barley, oats, wine grapes, potatoes, vegetables, citrus fruits, dates, figs, tobacco, olives, cork.	Clothing, shoes, wine, tobacco products, cement, paper, steel, lead pipe, copper wire, telephone cables, superphosphates, matches, lime.	Agriculture.............. Stock raising............
ARGENTINA	Petroleum, coal, tungsten, mica, beryl, lead, antimony, bismuth, chromite, columbite-tantalite, copper, gold, silver.	Wheat, corn, oats, barley, rye, oilseeds, sugar cane, cotton, citrus and other fruits, vegetables, animal & dairy products.	Meat & dairy products, machinery, flour, brewery products, rubber goods, textiles, leather goods, cement, refined oil, vegetable oils, quebracho extract.	Agriculture.............. Stock raising............ Manufacturing. ....
AUSTRALIA	Gold, coal, iron ore, silver, lead, copper, zinc, arsenic, gypsum, limestone, magnesite, salt, tin ore.	Pastoral & dairy products, wheat, oats, corn, barley, hay, sugar cane, fruits, pumpkins, melons, potatoes.	Industrial metals & machinery, foods, beverages, tobacco, clothing, textiles & products, chemicals, paper, printing, woodwork, leather, bricks, pottery, glass, rubber, furniture.	Manufacturing......31.0 Agriculture........17.5 Government, professions.11.4 Transportation, communications......8.8 Service.............7.7
BELGIUM	Coal, zinc, lead, silver, copper, gold, palladium, nickel, tin, antimony, cadmium, iron ore.	Grains, sugar beets, flaxseed, tubers, vegetables, fruits, hops, tobacco, hay crops, livestock, poultry.	Dairy products, textiles, clothing, petroleum products, chemicals, ceramic, metal goods, machinery, leather, tobacco products.	Industry...........55.0 Agricultural & forestry...17.0 Trade.............14.0 Domestic&household work5.0 Professions..........4.0
BRAZIL	Iron ore, coal, gold, quartz crystal, manganese, silver, zirconium sand, mica, diamonds, marble, semi-precious stones, petroleum, chromite.	Coffee, corn, rice, cotton, sugar, manioc, beans, fruits, potatoes, wheat, cacao, tobacco, cottonseed, castor beans, livestock.	Foodstuffs, textiles & yarns, clothing, chemicals, pharmaceuticals, iron & steel, metal products, wood products, glass, ceramics, building materials, paper & printing, rubber goods, leather products.	Domestic activities & students..........41.0 Agriculture, fishing, etc.35.0 Manufacturing........6.0 Social services & activities 4.0 Commerce..........3.0 Transportation & communication......2.0
BULGARIA	Lignite, coal, iron ore, salt, kaolin, chromium, manganese, lead, zinc &	Wheat, corn, potatoes, tobacco, sugar beets, barley, oats, rye, livestock, poultry.	Textiles, cement, rose oil, tobacco products, flour.	Agriculture & fishing...74.3 Industry...........9.8 Commerce...........4.8

Country	Minerals	Agricultural products	Manufactured products	Occupations (%)
(continued)	copper ores, kieselguhr, gold, antimony			Public administration 3.2 Professions 2.6 Military 1.5
CANADA	Gold, coal, nickel, copper, zinc, platinum, asbestos, lead, petroleum, natural gas, silver, gypsum, sulphur, quartz, cobalt, arsenic, iron ore.	Wheat, oats, barley, flax, other grains, hay & forage, potatoes, vegetables, tobacco, sugar beets, fruits, dairy products, livestock, poultry.	Paper, wood products, vegetable products, animal products, textiles, clothing, metal products, nonmetallic mineral products, chemicals.	Manufacturing 27.0 Agriculture 24.0 Services 17.0 Trade & finance 15.0 Transportation & communication 8.0 Construction 5.0
CHILE	Copper, nitrates, iodine, coal, gold, silver, manganese, borates, iron ore, sulphur, petroleum, cobalt, lead, mercury.	Wheat, beans, grapes & other fruits, potatoes, barley, rice, corn, oats, peas, vegetable oils & oil seeds, tobacco, hemp, livestock.	Textiles, tobacco products, glass, leather goods, foodstuffs, wine, pharmaceuticals, paper, cement, explosives, wood products, pipe & steel.	Agriculture 33.9 Industry & construction 24.7 Commerce 12.2 Mining 5.9 Fishing 0.4
CHINA	Coal, antimony, tungsten, gold, silver, iron ore, pyrites, copper, tin, petroleum.	Wheat, millet, kaoliang, rice, corn, peanuts, grain sorghum, silk, tung oil, tobacco, cotton, soybeans, rapeseed, sugar cane, tea.	Cotton textiles, clothing, silk, cement, ceramics, sugar, chemical products, tobacco, foodstuffs, leather & rubber goods, furniture, machinery, paper & printing.	Agriculture 80.0
COLOMBIA	Petroleum, gold, silver, platinum, salt, coal, lead, barite, gypsum, emeralds.	Coffee, corn, potatoes, yuca, plantains & bananas, wheat, rice, copra, cacao, tobacco, cotton, barley.	Textiles & clothing, tobacco products, leather, pharmaceuticals, beverages, metal products, petroleum products, sugar, cement.	Agriculture 74.0 Industry 12.0 Commerce & trade 3.0 Mining & quarrying 1.0
CZECHOSLO-VAKIA	Coal, iron ore, petroleum, graphite, silver, lead, zinc, copper, manganese ore, salt, tin, pyrites, wolfram.	Potatoes, sugar beets, wheat, rye, oats, barley, corn, tobacco, peas, beans, hops, grapes, oilseeds.	Iron & steel products, chemicals, glass, wood products, textiles, clothing, hides, leather, rubber goods, sugar, beer, metal goods.	Crafts, trades 32.2 Agriculture, forestry & fishing 29.7 Public service, administration 6.9 Transportation 6.1 Commerce, banking 6.0
DENMARK	Limestone, clay.	Butter, beef, veal, pork, eggs, cheese, grains, potatoes, fodder roots, beets, fish products, sugar.	Processed foods, iron & steel products, machinery, textiles, clothing, earthenware, wood products, leather products, paper & printing.	Industry & handicraft 33.0 Agriculture & fishing 28.0 Commerce, banking, insurance 13.0 Public service, arts & science 7.0 Transportation, communications 6.0

ECONOMIC FACTS FOR PRINCIPAL COUNTRIES (Continued)

Country	Mineral Resources	Principal Agricultural Products	Principal Manufactures	Principal Occupations % of Total Employed
EGYPT	Phosphate rock, petroleum, gypsum, salt, pumice, copper, iron, chromium ore, manganese ore, gold.	Cotton, sugar cane, rice, corn, potatoes, fruits, barley, tobacco, vegetables, wheat, animal products.	Refined sugar, tobacco products, processed foods, leather goods, soap, cotton goods, furniture, paper products, vegetable oils, cement.	Agriculture............75.0
FRANCE	Iron ore, coal, sulphur, potash, petroleum, bauxite, lead, zinc, antimony, iron pyrites.	Wheat, rye, oats, barley, corn, buckwheat, grapes, fruits, berries, nuts, root crops, silkworms, meat & dairy products.	Metal products, machinery, automotive equipment, food products, wine, chemicals, textiles, wood products, rubber products, leather, paper, metallurgical products.	Agriculture, forestry, fishing.............57.9 Industry............29.0 Transport............5.0 Banking, insurance......1.9 Mining, quarrying......1.3
GERMANY	Coal, phosphates, potash, petroleum, lead, zinc, copper, gypsum.	Sugar beets, barley, rye, oats, wheat, oilseeds, root crops, hemp, tobacco, hay, hops, fruits, nuts, grapes, animal products.	Iron & steel, hardware, machinery, vehicles, textiles, rubber goods, leather goods, wood products, ceramics, chemicals, glass.	Industry & handicrafts...42.0 Agriculture & forestry...25.0 Communications & transportation.......17.0 Public & private service..13.0 Domestic service........3.0
GREAT BRITAIN AND N. IRELAND	Coal, iron ore, lead, tin, barite, zinc, limestone.	Potatoes, sugar beets, oats, wheat, barley, hay, vegetables, turnips, swedes, mangels, fruit, flax, hops.	Metal products, machinery, motors, transportation equipment, foodstuffs, textiles, clothing, leather, chemicals, china & glassware, ships, paper, wood products, fertilizers.	Manufacturing........37.6 Trade............11.5 Commerce, finance, professions, services......10.4 Government service....10.2 Transport............7.0
GREECE	Magnesite, iron pyrites, lead, emery, chrome ore, iron ore, nickel & zinc ore, bauxite, lignite.	Wheat & other grains, tobacco, fruits, olives, cotton, potatoes, grapes, dairy products, animal products.	Textiles, chemicals, foodstuffs, leather goods, machinery, building materials, wood products, clothing, tobacco, metal products.	Agriculture & service............60.0-65.0 Industry & manufacturing........18.0 Commerce & transport...15.0 Free professions......... Government departments....
HUNGARY	Bauxite, petroleum, lignite & coal, iron ore,	Corn, potatoes, wheat, sugar beets, rye, vegetables,	Food products, wine, textiles, clothing, iron & metal goods,	Agriculture, forestry & fishing............52.0

	Minerals	Agricultural Products	Manufactures	Occupations
	mangnaese ore, natural gas, quarry products.	onions, barley, grapes, hemp, animal products.	machinery, chemicals, leather goods, stone, earthenware, glass.	Mining & industry....23.0 Public service, professions, domestic service, etc....15.7 Communications....3.9
INDIA	Coal, gold, salt, mica manganese ore, petroleum, iron ore, copper ore, ilmenite, steatite, saltpetre, china clay, fireclay.	Rice, wheat, millet, barley, corn, pulses, cotton, peanuts, sesamum, rape, mustard, linseed, castorseed, nuts, tea, sugar, jute, coffee, tapioca, rubber.	Cotton textiles, iron & steel products, glass, chemicals, leather goods, electrical goods, jute manufactures, sugar, tea, refined petroleum, carpets, cement, paper & wood products.	Agriculture....73.0 Commerce & professions..16.0 Cottage industries.....9.0 Organized industries....1.5
INDONESIA	Petroleum, tin ore, bauxite, coal, salt, nickel, manganese.	Rubber, copra, spices, sugar, tea, coffee, rice, tobacco, soybeans, sisal, kapok, cassava, cacao.	Textiles, paper, soap, glassware, rubber goods, foodstuffs, beverages, tobacco, chemicals, metal products, quinine.	Production of raw materials......68.8 Industry.........10.6 Domestic service....9.6 Commerce........6.2 Public administration...2.5
IRAN (PERSIA)	Petroleum, salt, red oxide of iron, coal, copper, lead, zinc, antimony, manganese, sulphur, gold.	Wheat, barley, rice, corn, cotton, wool, dates, apricots, grapes, sugar beets, tobacco, opium, nuts, tea.	Carpets, textiles, food products, beverages, tobacco products, refined oil, sugar, leather, glass, cement, matches.	Agriculture & stock raising..........85.0
ISRAEL	Magnesiumbromide, chlorides (sodium, potassium, calcium, magnesium), limestone, sand, barite.	Cereals, citrus fruits, olives, grapes, vegetables, poultry, livestock.	Processed foods, textiles, cut diamonds, chemicals, leather goods, metal products, machine tools, cement, books.	(Jewish only) Manufacturing......27.8 Agriculture........14.8 Commerce & trade....10.9
ITALY	Coal, lignite, iron ore, mercury, lead, zinc, bauxite, copper, pyrites, talc, barite, sulphur, marble, pumice, magnesium.	Wheat, corn, rice, other cereals, potatoes, sugar beets, grapes, citrus & other fruits, olives, nuts, silk, wool, hemp, flax.	Food products, textiles, chemicals, metal products, cement, glass, automobiles, rubber goods, leather goods, footwear, ceramics, paints, wood & paper products.	Agriculture, forestry, fishing.........48.2 Manufacturing......28.6 Commerce, banking, insurance........8.8 Public & private administration......4.8 Transport & communication....3.8 Domestic service......3.6
JAPAN	Coal, lignite, petroleum, iron pyrites, silver, copper, gold, zinc, sulphur, tin, mercury.	Rice, wheat, oats, barley, sweet potatoes, white potatoes, tea, tobacco, pyrethrum, silkworms.	Textiles, iron & steel products, machinery, chemicals, electrical goods, footwear, cement, vehicles, ships, glass, paper, cameras, handicraft articles.	Agriculture........... Industry.............

ECONOMIC FACTS FOR PRINCIPAL COUNTRIES (*Continued*)

Country	Mineral Resources	Principal Agricultural Products	Principal Manufactures	Principal Occupations % of Total Employed
MEXICO	Silver, gold, lead, zinc, copper, petroleum, iron ore, tin, mercury, antimony, manganese, tungsten, molybdenum, cadmium, arsenic, coal, mica.	Corn, cotton, sugar cane, wheat, henequen, bananas, sesame, fruits, vegetables, coffee, beans, rice, tobacco, livestock.	Textiles, clothing, flour, beverages, beer, soap, vegetable oils, tobacco, iron & steel products, glass, furniture, chemicals, ceramics, leather goods, rubber products, handicraft articles.	Agriculture........65.5 Industry..........10.9 Trade.............9.4 Public service......3.2 Domestic service....3.0 Communications.....2.6 Mining, petroleum...1.9
NETHERLANDS	Coal, salt, petroleum.	Wheat, pulses, root crops, sugar beets, fruits, vegetables, rye, oats, barley, animal products.	Food products, metal products & machinery, electrical equipment, chemical products, textiles, footwear & leather, rubber goods.	Industry.........39.0 Commerce & trade...28.0 Agriculture.......20.0
NORWAY	Iron ore, copper, molybdenum, pyrites, rutile, zinc, lead, sulphur, nickel, silver.	Oats, potatoes, barley, wheat, hay & other forage, rye, vegetables, fruits, livestock, poultry.	Iron & metal products, processed foods, beverages, & tobacco, wood products, textiles, clothing, refined ores & metals, chemical products, publications, processed fish.	Agriculture & forestry ..33.0 Industry..........30.5 Commerce & transportation.......21.7 Fishing............7.7 Service & professions.....6.1 Domestic service....1.0
PAKISTAN	Coal, chrome ore, petroleum, salt, limestone, gypsum, clay.	Wheat, rice, cotton, jute, tea, barley, pulses, oil seeds, tobacco, sugar cane, millet, animal products.	Cotton textiles, sugar, cement, foundry products, flour, petroleum products.	Agriculture........85.0 Crafts & cottage industries.......4.0 Organized industries..under1.0
POLAND	Coal, lignite, zinc, lead, iron ore, nickel, phosphates, salt, petroleum, potash.	Potatoes, rye, sugar beets, oats, barley, wheat, peas, beans, rapeseed, flaxseed, hemp.	Processed foods, flour, metal goods, wood products, chemicals, textiles, clothing, paper, building materials.	Agriculture........ Industry.......... Mining............ Government service....
ROMANIA	Petroleum, natural gas, lignite, coal, iron ore, lead, zinc, gold, silver, chrome ore, bauxite, manganese, copper, salt, talc.	Corn, wheat, flax, hemp, sugar beets, potatoes, oats, barley, rye, tobacco, vegetables, fruits, animal products.	Metallurgical products, textiles, flour, beer, chemicals, wood & paper products, leather, building material, publications, petroleum products.	Agriculture........80.0 Industry...........9.0
SOUTH AFRICA	Gold, diamonds, coal, copper, manganese ore,	Corn, wheat, oats, barley, rye, potatoes, sugar cane,	Processed food, beverages & tobacco, iron & steel, metal prod-	Agriculture........ Mining............

Country	Minerals	Agricultural products	Manufactured products	Occupation (%)
	chrome ore, asbestos, platinum, corundum, granite, iron pyrites.	tobacco, fruits, peanuts, cotton, sunflower seed, wool, animal products.	ducts, clothing & textiles, chemicals, fertilizers, leather goods, books, vehicles, wood products.	Manufacturing....••
SOVIET UNION	Coal, petroleum, natural gas, peat, iron ore, manganese ore, chrome ore, platinum, iridium, palladium, osmium, asbestos.	Wheat, oats, barley, rye, flax, cotton, rice, tea, tobacco, grapes, citrus fruits, vegetables, potatoes, sugar beets.	Metallurgical products, textiles, chemicals, foodstuffs, leather goods.	Agriculture....60.0 Manufacturing....11.0 Handicrafts....4.0 Construction....2.0
SPAIN	Coal, iron ore, lime, iron pyrites, copper & copper pyrites, salt, lead, zinc, tin, tungsten, mercury, potash, fluorspar, sulphur.	Cereals, olives, legumes, grapes, root crops, vegetables, cork, nuts, sugar beets, oranges & other fruits, tobacco.	Iron & steel, textiles, chemicals, pharmaceuticals, electrical equipment, shoes & leather products, cement, canned fish.	Agriculture....•••• Mining....•••• Textile manufacturing....•••
SWEDEN	Iron ore, gold, silver, lead, copper, zinc, pyrites, tungsten, manganese, molybdenum, antimony.	Wheat, oats, rye, barley, potatoes, sugar beets, oil & fiber plants, dairy products, poultry products, meat.	Mechanical wood pulp, chemical wood pulp, paper, sinter, ingot metal, iron & steel, superphosphates, woolen cloth, cotton cloth.	Industry & handicrafts..36.0 Agriculture....32.0 Trade....11.0 Public administration & free professions....8.0
TURKEY	Chromite, iron ore, coal, copper, salt, sulphur, asbestos, antimony, boracite, manganese, emery.	Cereals, raisin grapes, figs, tobacco, olives, cotton, nuts, vegetables, flax, opium, livestock products.	Processed agricultural products, textiles, yarn, ceramics, cellulose products, chemicals, metal products, leather, rugs & carpets.	Agriculture....82.0 Mining & industry....8.0 Commerce, transportation, etc....5.0 Public service, professions, etc....5.0
UNITED STATES (excluding Alaska)	Petroleum, coal, iron ore, natural gas, stone, natural gasoline, ferro-alloys, copper, sand & gravel, clay, zinc, sulphur, gold, lime, lead, salt, potassium, phosphate rock, silver.	Corn, hay, cotton, wheat, vegetables, oats, tobacco, legumes, potatoes, citrus fruits, sorghum, apples, barley, grapes, peaches, rice, nuts, sugar beets, pears, livestock & products.	Processed foods, beverages, & tobacco, textiles, clothing, metal products, transport equipment, printing, chemicals, machinery, petroleum products, lumber & wood products, electrical equipment, glass & china, leather goods.	Manufacturing....23.4 Agriculture, forestry, fishing....18.8 Wholesale & retail trade..16.7 Personal services....8.9 Professions & related services....7.4
YUGOSLAVIA	Iron ore, bauxite, coal, antimony, pyrites, chrome ore, lead, copper, zinc, petroleum, manganese, gold.	Corn, oats, barley, wheat, rye, beets, fruits, hemp, tobacco, dairy products, sugar beets, potatoes, flax, hops, livestock products.	Processed foods, textiles, matches, chemicals, cement, light manufactures, light metallurgical products, leather, paper, sugar.	Agriculture....76.3 Industry....10.7 Public service....4.5 Trade & distribution....4.0

GEOGRAPHICAL FACTS ABOUT THE U.S.

ELEVATION

Highest: Mount McKinley, Alsk., 20,320 feet.
Lowest: Death Valley, Calif., 282 feet below sea level.
Average: 2,500 feet.

EXTREMITIES

Northernmost: Point Barrow, Alsk.
Southernmost: South Cape, Haw.
Easternmost: West Quoddy Head, near Eastport, Maine.
Westernmost: Cape Wrangell, Attu Island, Alsk.
The two places in the United States separated by the greatest distance are Kure Island, Haw., and Mangrove Point, Fla. These points are approximately 5,848 miles apart.

LENGTH OF U.S. BOUNDARIES

U. S.-Canadian boundary: 5,360 miles.
U. S.-Mexican boundary: 2,013 miles.
Atlantic coastline: 5,565 miles.
Pacific and Arctic coastline: 9,272 miles.
Gulf of Mexico coastline: 3,641 miles.
Total length of all U. S. coastlines and land boundaries: 25,851 miles.

GEOGRAPHIC CENTERS

Geographic center of the continental United States (including Alaska and Hawaii) is in Butte County, S. Dak., at 44°58'N., 103°46'W.
Geographic center of North America is near Devils Lake, N. Dak., at 48°10'N., 100°10'W.

EXTREMES OF TEMPERATURE

Highest temperature ever recorded: 134°F., at Greenland Ranch, Death Valley, Calif., on July 10, 1913.
Lowest temperature ever recorded: −78°F., at Fort Yukon, Alsk., on Jan. 14, 1934.

PRECIPITATION

Average annual precipitation: Approximately 29 inches.
Wettest state: Hawaii, with an average annual rainfall of 82.48 inches.
Driest state: Nevada, with an average annual rainfall of 8.81 inches.
The greatest local average annual rainfall in the United States is at Mt. Waialeale, Kauai, Haw., 472 inches.
Greatest 24-hour rainfall: 23.22 inches at New Smyrna, Fla., Oct. 10-11, 1924.
Extreme minimum rainfall records in the United States include a total fall of only 3.93 inches at Bagdad, Calif., for a period of 5 years, 1909-13, and an annual average of 1.35 inches at Greenland Ranch, Death Valley, Calif.
Heavy snowfall records include 60 inches at Giant Forest, Calif., in 1 day; 42 inches at Angola, N. Y., in 2 days; 54 inches at The Dalles, Oreg., in 3 days; and 96 inches at Vanceboro, Maine, in 4 days.
Greatest seasonal snowfall: 884 inches, more than 73 feet, at Tamarack, Calif., during the winter of 1906-7.

HISTORICAL FACTS ABOUT THE U.S.

TERRITORIAL ACQUISITIONS

Accession	Date	Area (sq. mi.)	Cost in Dollars
Original territory of the Thirteen States..............	1790	888,811	....
Purchase of Louisiana Territory, from France..........	1803	827,192	$11,250,000.00
By treaty with Spain: Florida........................	1819	58,560	$ 5,000,000.00
Other areas..................	1819	13,443	....
Annexation of Texas.................................	1845	390,144	....
Oregon Territory, by treaty with Great Britain........	1846	285,580	....
Mexican Cession.....................................	1848	529,017	$15,000,000.00
Gadsden Purchase, from Mexico.......................	1853	29,640	$10,000,000.00
Purchase of Alaska, from Russia......................	1867	586,400	7,200,000.00
Annexation of Hawaiian Islands......................	1898	6,424	....
Puerto Rico, by treaty with Spain....................	1898	3,435	....
Guam, by treaty with Spain..........................	1898	206	....
American Samoa, by treaty, with Great Britain and Germany..	1900	76	....
Panama Canal Zone, by treaty with Panama............	1904	553	*$10,000,000.00
Corn Islands (leased)................................	1914	4	....
Virgin Islands, by purchase from Denmark.............	1917	133	$25,000,000.00
Minor Islands.......................................	......	42	....
Total.......................		3,619,660	$83,450,000.00

Note: The Philippines, ceded by Spain in 1898 for $20,000,000.00, were a territorial possession of the United States from 1898 to 1946. On July 4, 1946, they became the independent republic of the Philippines.

* $25,000,000.00 was also paid to the republic of Columbia, out of whose territory the republic of Panama was created. In addition, an annual payment of $1,930,000.00 is made to the republic of Panama.

WESTWARD MOVEMENT OF CENTER OF POPULATION

Year	U.S. Population Total of Census	Approximate Location
1790	3,929,214	23 miles E. of Baltimore, Md.
1800	5,308,483	18 miles W. of Baltimore, Md.
1810	7,239,881	40 miles N.W. of Washington, D.C.
1820	9,638,453	16 miles E. of Moorefield, W. Va.
1830	12,866,020	19 miles S.W. of Moorefield, W. Va.
1840	17,069,453	16 miles S. of Clarksburg,W. Va.
1850	23,191,876	23 miles S.E. of Parkersburg, W. Va.
1860	31,443,321	20 miles S.E. of Chillicothe, Ohio
1870	39,818,449	48 miles N.E. of Cincinnati, Ohio
1880	50,155,783	8 miles S.W. of Cincinnati, Ohio
1890	62,947,714	20 miles E. of Columbus, Ind.
1900	75,994,575	6 miles S.E. of Columbus, Ind.
1910	91,972,266	Bloomington, Ind.
1920	105,710,620	8 miles S.E. of Spencer, Ind.
1930	122,775,046	3 miles N.E. of Linton, Ind.
1940	131,669,275	2 miles S.E. of Carlisle, Ind.
1950	150,697,361	8 miles N.W. of Olney, Ill.
1960	179,323,175	6 miles N.W. of Centralia, Ill.

235

STATE	Land Area (square miles) in 1960	Water Area (square miles) in 1960	Total Area (square miles) in 1960
Alabama..................	51,060	549	51,609
Alaska...................	571,065	15,335	586,400
Arizona..................	113,575	334	113,909
Arkansas................	52,499	605	53,104
California	156,573	2,120	158,693
Colorado................	103,884	363	104,247
Connecticut.............	4,899	110	5,009
Delaware................	1,978	79	2,057
District of Columbia†.......	61	8	69
Florida..................	54,252	4,308	58,560
Georgia.................	58,274	602	58,876
Hawaii..................	6,415	9	6,424
Idaho...................	82,708	849	83,557
Illinois.................	55,930	470	56,400
Indiana.................	36,185	106	36,291
Iowa...................	56,032	258	56,290
Kansas.................	82,048	216	82,264
Kentucky...............	39,863	532	40,395
Louisiana...............	45,106	3,417	48,523
Maine..................	31,012	2,203	33,215
Maryland...............	9,874	703	10,577
Massachusetts...........	7,867	390	8,257
Michigan................	57,019	1,197	58,216
Minnesota...............	80,009	4,059	84,068
Mississippi..............	47,223	493	47,716
Missouri................	69,138	548	69,686
Montana................	145,736	1,402	147,138
Nebraska...............	76,612	615	77,227
Nevada.................	109,788	752	110,540
New Hampshire..........	9,014	290	9,304
New Jersey..............	7,521	315	7,836
New Mexico.............	121,510	156	121,666
New York	47,939	1,637	49,576
North Carolina..........	49,067	3,645	52,712
North Dakota	69,457	1,208	70,665
Ohio...................	40,972	250	41,222
Oklahoma...............	68,887	1,032	69,919
Oregon.................	96,248	733	96,981
Pennsylvania............	45,007	326	45,333
Rhode Island...........	1,058	156	1,214
South Carolina..........	30,272	783	31,055
South Dakota	76,378	669	77,047
Tennessee..............	41,762	482	42,244
Texas..................	262,840	4,499	267,339
Utah...................	82,339	2,577	84,916
Vermont................	9,276	333	9,609
Virginia................	39,838	977	40,815
Washington.............	66,709	1,483	68,192
West Virginia	24,079	102	24,181
Wisconsin	54,705	1,449	56,154
Wyoming...............	97,411	503	97,914
United States...........	3,548,974	66,237	3,675,633*

† District. * Includes the United States parts of the Great Lakes (60,422 square miles). These are not included in state figures.

Rank in Area	Population in 1960	Population Per Square Mile in 1960	Rank in Population in 1960	Rank in Population in 1950
29	3,266,740	63	19	17
1	226,167	.04	50	50
6	1,302,161	11	35	37
27	1,786,272	34	31	30
3	15,717,204	99	2	2
8	1,753,947	17	33	34
48	2,535,234	506	25	28
49	446,292	217	46	47
..	763,956	11,072	..	..
22	4,951,560	85	10	20
21	3,943,116	67	16	13
47	632,772	99	43	45
13	667,191	8	42	43
24	10,081,158	179	4	4
38	4,662,498	128	11	12
25	2,757,537	49	24	22
14	2,178,611	26	28	31
37	3,038,156	75	22	19
31	3,257,022	67	20	21
39	969,265	29	36	35
42	3,100,689	293	21	23
45	5,148,578	624	9	9
23	7,823,194	134	7	7
12	3,413,864	41	18	18
32	2,178,141	46	29	26
19	4,319,813	62	13	11
4	674,767	4.6	41	42
15	1,411,330	18	34	33
7	285,278	2.6	49	49
44	606,921	65	45	44
46	6,066,782	774	8	8
5	951,023	7.8	37	39
30	16,782,304	339	1	1
28	4,556,155	86	12	10
17	632,446	8.9	44	41
35	9,706,397	235	5	5
18	2,328,284	33	27	25
10	1,768,687	18	32	32
33	11,319,366	250	3	3
50	859,488	708	39	36
40	2,382,594	77	26	27
16	680,514	8.8	40	40
34	3,567,089	84	17	16
2	9,579,677	36	6	6
11	890,627	10	38	38
43	389,881	41	47	46
36	3,966,949	97	14	15
20	2,853,214	42	23	24
41	1,860,421	77	30	29
26	3,951,777	70	15	14
9	330,066	3.4	48	48
..	179,323,175	49	..	..

U.S. STATE GENERAL INFORMATION TABLE

State	Capital	Largest City	Date of Entry	Rank of Entry	State Flower	State Nickname
Alabama	Montgomery	Birmingham	Dec. 14, 1819	22	Camellia	Cotton
Alaska	Juneau	Anchorage	January, 1959	49	Forget-me-not	Last Frontier
Arizona	Phoenix	Phoenix	Feb. 14, 1912	48	Saguaro Cactus	Grand Canyon
Arkansas	Little Rock	Little Rock	June 15, 1836	25	Apple Blossom	Wonder
California	Sacramento	Los Angeles	Sept. 9, 1850	31	Golden Poppy	Golden
Colorado	Denver	Denver	Aug. 1, 1876	38	Rocky Mountain Columbine	Centennial
Connecticut*	Hartford	Hartford	Jan. 9, 1788	5	Mountain Laurel	Constitution
Delaware*	Dover	Wilmington	Dec. 7, 1787	1	Peach Blossom	Diamond
District of Columbia†	Washington	Washington	March 3, 1791	..	American Beauty Rose	....
Florida	Tallahassee	Miami	March 3, 1845	27	Orange Blossom	Sunshine
Georgia*	Atlanta	Atlanta	Jan. 2, 1788	4	Cherokee Rose	Cracker
Hawaii	Honolulu	Honolulu	August, 1959	50	Red Hibiscus	The Aloha
Idaho	Boise	Boise	July 3, 1890	43	Syringa	Gem
Illinois	Springfield	Chicago	Dec. 3, 1818	21	Native Violet	Prairie
Indiana	Indianapolis	Indianapolis	Dec. 11, 1816	19	Peony	Hoosier
Iowa	Des Moines	Des Moines	Dec. 28, 1846	29	Wild Rose	Hawkeye
Kansas	Topeka	Wichita	Jan. 29, 1861	34	Sunflower	Sunflower
Kentucky	Frankfort	Louisville	June 1, 1792	15	Goldenrod	Bluegrass
Louisiana	Baton Rouge	New Orleans	April 30, 1812	18	Magnolia	Pelican
Maine	Augusta	Portland	March 15, 1820	23	White Pine Cone & Tassel	Pine Tree
Maryland*	Annapolis	Baltimore	April 28, 1788	7	Black-eyed Susan	Old Line
Massachusetts*	Boston	Boston	Feb. 6, 1788	6	Mayflower	Bay
Michigan	Lansing	Detroit	Jan. 26, 1837	26	Apple Blossom	Wolverine
Minnesota	St. Paul	Minneapolis	May 11, 1858	32	Showy Lady-slipper	Gopher
Mississippi	Jackson	Jackson	Dec. 10, 1817	20	Magnolia	Magnolia

State	Capital	City	Date	No.	Flower		Nickname
Missouri	Jefferson City	St. Louis	Aug. 10, 1821	24	Hawthorne		Show-Me
Montana	Helena	Great Falls	Nov. 8, 1889	41	Bitterroot		Treasure
Nebraska	Lincoln	Omaha	March 1, 1867	37	Goldenrod		Cornhusker
Nevada	Carson City	Las Vegas	Oct. 31, 1864	36	Sagebrush		Silver
New Hampshire*	Concord	Manchester	June 21, 1788	9	Purple Lilac		Granite
New Jersey*	Trenton	Newark	Dec. 18, 1787	3	Purple Violet		Garden
New Mexico*	Santa Fe	Albuquerque	Jan. 6, 1912	47	Yucca		Land of Enchantment
New York*	Albany	New York	July 26, 1788	11	Rose		Empire
North Carolina*	Raleigh	Charlotte	Nov. 21, 1789	12	Dogwood		Tar Heel
North Dakota	Bismarck	Fargo	Nov. 2, 1889	39	Wild Prairie Rose		Flickertail
Ohio	Columbus	Cleveland	March 1, 1803	17	Scarlet Carnation		Buckeye
Oklahoma	Oklahoma City	Oklahoma City	Nov. 16, 1907	46	Mistletoe		Sooner
Oregon*	Salem	Portland	Feb. 14, 1859	33	Oregon Grape		Beaver
Pennsylvania*	Harrisburg	Philadelphia	Dec. 12, 1787	2	Mountain Laurel		Keystone
Rhode Island*	Providence	Providence	May 29, 1790	13	Violet**		Little Rhody
South Carolina*	Columbia	Columbia	May 23, 1788	8	Carolina Jessamine		Palmetto
South Dakota	Pierre	Sioux Falls	Nov. 2, 1889	40	American Pasque Flower		Coyote
Tennessee*	Nashville	Memphis	June 1, 1796	16	Iris		Volunteer
Texas	Austin	Houston	Dec. 29, 1845	28	Bluebonnet		Lone Star
Utah	Salt Lake City	Salt Lake City	Jan. 4, 1896	45	Sego Lily		Beehive
Vermont*	Montpelier	Burlington	March 4, 1791	14	Red Clover		Green Mountain
Virginia*	Richmond	Norfolk	June 26, 1788	10	American Dogwood		Old Dominion
Washington	Olympia	Seattle	Nov. 11, 1889	42	Western Rhododendron		Evergreen
West Virginia*	Charleston	Charleston	June 20, 1863	35	Rhododendron		Mountain
Wisconsin	Madison	Milwaukee	May 29, 1848	30	Wood Violet		Badger
Wyoming	Cheyenne	Cheyenne	July 10, 1890	44	Indian Paint Brush		Equality
United States	Washington, D.C.	New York	....	..	....		....

*One of the Thirteen Original States.   **Unofficial.   †District.

STATES	1650	1770	1800	1860	1900	1920	1930	1940	1950	1960
Alabama	.....	.....	.....	964,201	1,828,697	2,348,174	2,646,248	2,832,961	3,061,743	3,266,740
Alaska	.....	.....	.....	.....	63,592	55,036	59,278	72,524	128,643	226,167
Arizona	.....	.....	.....	.....	122,931	334,162	435,573	499,261	749,587	1,302,161
Arkansas	.....	.....	.....	435,450	1,311,564	1,752,204	1,854,482	1,949,387	1,909,511	1,786,272
California	.....	.....	.....	379,994	1,485,053	3,426,861	5,677,251	6,907,387	10,586,223	15,717,204
Colorado	.....	.....	.....	34,277	539,700	939,629	1,035,791	1,123,296	1,325,089	1,753,947
Connecticut	4,139	183,881	251,002	460,147	908,420	1,380,631	1,606,903	1,709,242	2,007,280	2,535,234
Delaware	185	35,496	64,273	112,216	184,735	223,003	238,380	266,505	318,085	446,292
District of Columbia	.....	.....	8,144	75,080	278,718	437,571	486,869	663,091	802,178	763,956
Florida	.....	.....	.....	140,424	528,542	968,470	1,468,211	1,897,414	2,771,305	4,951,560
Georgia	.....	23,375	162,686	1,057,286	2,216,331	2,895,832	2,908,506	3,123,723	3,444,578	3,943,116
Hawaii	.....	.....	.....	.....	154,001	255,881	368,300	423,330	499,794	632,772
Idaho	.....	.....	.....	.....	161,772	431,866	445,032	524,873	588,637	667,191
Illinois	.....	.....	.....	1,711,951	4,821,550	5,485,280	7,630,654	7,897,241	8,712,176	10,081,158
Indiana	.....	.....	5,641	1,350,428	2,516,462	2,930,390	3,238,503	3,427,796	3,934,224	4,662,498
Iowa	.....	.....	.....	674,913	2,231,853	2,404,021	2,470,939	2,538,268	2,621,073	2,757,537
Kansas	.....	.....	.....	107,206	1,470,495	1,769,257	1,880,999	1,801,028	1,905,299	2,178,611
Kentucky	.....	15,700	220,955	1,155,684	2,147,174	2,416,630	2,614,589	2,845,627	2,944,806	3,038,156
Louisiana	.....	.....	.....	708,002	1,381,625	1,798,509	2,101,593	2,363,880	2,683,516	3,257,022
Maine[3]	.....	31,257	151,719	628,279	694,466	768,014	797,423	847,226	913,774	969,265
Maryland[3]	4,504	202,599	341,548	687,049	1,188,044	1,449,661	1,631,526	1,821,244	2,343,001	3,100,689
Massachusetts[3]	16,603	235,308	422,845	1,231,066	2,805,346	3,852,356	4,249,614	4,316,721	4,690,514	5,148,578
Michigan	.....	.....	.....	749,113	2,420,982	3,668,412	4,842,325	5,256,106	6,371,766	7,823,194
Minnesota	.....	.....	.....	172,023	1,751,394	2,387,125	2,563,953	2,792,300	2,982,483	3,413,864
Mississippi	.....	.....	8,850	791,305	1,551,270	1,790,618	2,009,821	2,183,796	2,178,914	2,178,141
Missouri	.....	.....	.....	1,182,012	3,106,665	3,404,055	3,629,367	3,784,664	3,954,653	4,319,813
Montana	.....	.....	.....	.....	243,329	548,889	537,606	559,456	591,024	674,767
Nebraska	.....	.....	.....	28,841	1,066,300	1,296,372	1,377,963	1,315,834	1,325,510	1,411,330
Nevada	.....	.....	.....	6,857	42,335	77,407	91,058	110,247	160,083	285,278
New Hampshire	1,305	62,396	183,858	326,073	411,588	443,083	465,293	491,524	533,242	606,921

New Jersey	6,066,782	4,835,329	4,160,165	4,041,334	3,155,900	1,883,669	672,035	211,149	117,431	
New Mexico	951,023	681,187	531,818	423,317	360,350	195,310	93,516			
New York	16,782,304	14,830,192	13,479,142	12,588,066	10,385,227	7,268,894	3,880,735	589,051	162,920	4,166
North Carolina	4,556,155	4,061,929	3,571,623	3,170,276	2,559,123	1,893,810	992,622	478,103	197,200	
North Dakota[4]	632,446	619,636	641,935	680,845	646,872	319,146				
Ohio	9,706,397	7,946,627	6,907,612	6,646,697	5,759,394	4,157,545	2,339,511	45,365		
Oklahoma[5]	2,328,284	2,233,351	2,336,434	2,396,040	2,028,283	790,391				
Oregon	1,768,687	1,521,341	1,089,684	953,786	783,389	413,536	52,465			
Pennsylvania	11,319,366	10,498,012	9,900,180	9,631,350	8,720,017	6,302,115	2,906,215	602,365	240,057	
Rhode Island	859,488	791,896	713,346	687,497	604,397	428,556	174,620	69,122	58,196	785
South Carolina	2,382,594	2,117,027	1,899,804	1,738,765	1,683,724	1,340,316	703,708	345,591	124,244	
South Dakota[4]	680,514	652,740	642,961	692,849	636,547	401,570	4,837			
Tennessee	3,567,089	3,291,718	2,915,841	2,616,556	2,337,885	2,020,616	1,109,801	105,602	1,000	
Texas	9,579,677	7,711,194	6,414,824	5,824,715	4,663,228	3,048,710	604,215			
Utah	890,627	688,862	550,310	507,847	449,396	276,749	40,273			
Vermont	389,881	377,747	359,231	359,611	352,428	343,641	315,098	154,465	10,000	
Virginia[2]	3,966,949	3,318,680	2,677,773	2,421,851	2,309,187	1,854,184	1,219,630	807,557	447,016	18,731
Washington	2,853,214	2,378,963	1,736,191	1,563,396	1,356,621	518,103	11,594			
West Virginia[2]	1,860,421	2,005,552	1,901,974	1,729,205	1,463,701	958,800	376,688	78,592		
Wisconsin	3,951,777	3,434,575	3,137,587	2,939,006	2,632,067	2,069,042	775,881			
Wyoming	330,066	290,529	250,742	225,565	194,402	92,531				
Total[1]	179,323,175	151,325,798	132,164,569	123,202,624	106,021,537	76,212,168	31,443,321	5,308,483	2,148,076	50,368

[1] All figures exclude uncivilized Indians. Figures for 1650 and 1770 include the British colonies that later became the United States. No areas are included prior to their annexation to the United States. However, many of the figures refer to territories prior to their admission as States. U.S. total includes Alaska and Hawaii from 1900 through 1960.

[2] West Virginia figures for 1800 and 1860 are for that area of Virginia which became West Virginia in 1863. These figures are excluded from the figures for Virginia for 1800 and 1860.

[3] Maine figures for 1770 and 1800 are for that area of Massachusetts which became the State of Maine in 1820. Massachusetts figures exclude Maine in 1770 and 1800, but include it in 1650. Massachusetts figure for 1650 also includes Plymouth, a separate colony until 1691.

[4] South Dakota figure for 1860 represents entire Dakota Territory.

[5] Oklahoma figure for 1900 includes population of Indian Territory (392,060).

Rank 1960		Population 4/1/1960	Rank 1960		Population 4/1/1960
1	New York, N.Y......	15,404,300	44	Honolulu, Hawaii*.....	486,400
2	Los Angeles, Calif.....	6,565,000	45	Youngstown–Warren, Ohio..............	467,600
3	Chicago, Ill..........	6,517,600	46	San Bernardino–Riverside, Calif...........	460,000
4	Philadelphia, Pa.......	3,969,500	47	Jacksonville, Fla.......	456,700
5	Detroit, Mich.........	3,838,500	48	Oklahoma City, Okla.*.	448,300
	incl. part in Canada..	*4,028,500*	49	Syracuse, N.Y........	442,300
6	San Francisco–Oakland–San Jose, Calif.....	3,275,000	50	Omaha, Nebr.–Council Bluffs, Iowa........	434,800
7	Boston, Mass.*.......	2,913,500	51	Springfield–Holyoke, Mass..............	429,400
8	Cleveland, Ohio.......	2,090,800	52	Nashville, Tenn.*......	411,500
9	Washington, D.C.*....	2,053,600	53	Salt Lake City, Utah*..	410,200
10	St. Louis, Mo........	2,050,800	54	Richmond, Va.*......	409,100
11	Pittsburgh, Pa........	1,957,700	55	Flint, Mich..........	379,900
12	Baltimore, Md........	1,636,500	56	Grand Rapids, Mich...	367,300
13	Minneapolis–St. Paul,* Minn..............	1,441,700	57	Tulsa, Okla..........	360,900
14	Houston, Tex.........	1,251,700	58	Tampa, Fla..........	356,200
15	Buffalo–Niagara Falls, N.Y..............	1,244,200	59	St. Petersburg–Clearwater, Fla.........	355,200
	incl. part in Canada..	*1,330,000*	60	Wichita, Kans........	346,200
16	Milwaukee, Wis.......	1,240,700	61	Bridgeport, Conn......	322,800
17	Miami–Fort Lauderdale, Fla..........	1,212,000	62	New Haven, Conn.....	320,800
18	Cincinnati, Ohio......	1,203,300	63	Wilmington, Del......	318,700
19	Kansas City, Mo......	1,025,900	64	Worcester, Mass......	316,200
20	Dallas, Tex..........	1,022,300	65	El Paso, Tex.........	306,800
21	Atlanta, Ga.*........	1,011,100		*incl. part in Mexico..*	*599,000*
22	Seattle, Wash........	938,400	66	Mobile, Ala..........	304,000
23	San Diego, Calif.......	890,000	67	Allentown–Bethlehem, Pa................	299,700
	incl. part in Mexico..	*1,065,000*	68	Tacoma, Wash........	298,000
24	New Orleans, La......	885,200	69	Chattanooga, Tenn....	286,700
25	Denver, Colo.*.......	858,300	70	Knoxville–Oak Ridge, Tenn..............	286,000
26	Indianapolis, Ind.*....	806,900	71	Canton–Massillon, Ohio..............	281,900
27	Providence*–Pawtucket–Woonsocket, R.I....	804,300	72	Trenton, N.J.*........	279,800
28	Hartford*–New Britain, Conn..............	763,700	73	Charlotte, N.C........	272,700
29	Louisville, Ky........	735,800	74	Beaumont–Port Arthur, Tex..............	266,600
30	Portland, Oreg.......	731,200	75	Albuquerque, N. Mex..	266,300
31	Columbus, Ohio*.....	715,400	76	South Bend, Ind......	265,100
32	San Antonio, Tex.....	689,700	77	Peoria, Ill...........	265,000
33	Dayton, Ohio........	648,600	78	Des Moines, Iowa*....	261,900
34	Memphis, Tenn.......	628,100	79	Davenport, Iowa–Rock Island–Moline, Ill...	260,300
35	Birmingham, Ala......	624,000	80	Harrisburg, Pa.*......	257,600
36	Phoenix, Ariz.*.......	619,600	81	Orlando, Fla.........	255,800
37	Rochester, N.Y.......	594,500	82	Spokane, Wash.......	252,000
38	Albany*–Schenectady–Troy, N.Y..........	592,400	83	Wilkes-Barre, Pa.....	250,700
39	Norfolk–Portsmouth, Va..............	574,900	84	Baton Rouge, La.*....	248,700
40	Akron, Ohio.........	573,800	85	Shreveport, La........	245,200
41	Sacramento, Calif.*....	536,000	86	Tucson, Ariz..........	243,000
42	Toledo, Ohio.........	514,200			
43	Fort Worth, Tex......	505,100			

* *National or State capital.*
† *Metro. Areas are defined by Rand McNally & Company to provide as accurate*

Rank 1960	Population 4/1/1960	Rank 1960	Population 4/1/1960
87 Little Rock, Ark.*....	238,500	135 Colorado Springs, Colo...............	139,500
88 Huntington, W. Va.– Ashland, Ky......	231,100	136 Fall River, Mass.....	139,200
89 Fresno, Calif.........	228,000	137 Galveston–Texas City, Tex...............	138,700
90 Newport News– Hampton, Va......	219,200	138 Topeka, Kans.*......	135,800
91 Scranton, Pa........	215,600	139 Joliet, Ill............	132,100
92 Fort Wayne, Ind.....	215,400	140 Fayetteville, N.C.....	132,000
93 Charleston, W. Va.*...	213,900	141 Raleigh, N.C.*......	130,200
94 Columbia, S.C.*......	213,400	142 Atlantic City, N.J....	129,800
95 Binghamton, N.Y....	212,600	143 Waco, Tex...........	129,000
96 Pomona–Ontario, Calif...............	212,000	144 Lake Charles, La.....	127,200
97 Erie, Pa.............	212,000	145 Wheeling, W. Va.....	126,600
98 Austin, Tex.*.......	210,000	146 Johnstown, Pa.......	125,500
99 Lansing, Mich.*......	209,100	147 Lancaster, Pa........	125,100
100 Charleston, S.C......	203,100	148 Poughkeepsie, N.Y...	124,700
101 Columbus, Ga........	201,500	149 Gulfport–Biloxi, Miss.	124,200
102 Evansville, Ind.......	200,300	150 Lexington, Ky.......	124,000
103 Lawrence–Haverhill, Mass..............	196,500	151 Appleton, Wis........	123,200
104 Corpus Christi, Tex...	195,200	152 Springfield, Ill.*......	122,700
105 Reading, Pa.........	192,500	153 Eugene, Oreg.......	122,200
106 Jackson, Miss.*......	191,200	154 Jackson, Mich........	121,400
107 Rockford, Ill.........	191,100	155 Steubenville, Ohio– Weirton, W. Va....	121,300
108 Waterbury, Conn.....	190,300	156 Cedar Rapids, Iowa...	119,600
109 Savannah, Ga.......	189,200	157 Las Vegas, Nev......	119,300
110 Winston-Salem, N.C..	185,700	158 Wichita Falls, Tex....	116,900
111 Madison, Wis.*.......	179,200	159 Waterloo, Iowa......	114,300
112 Macon, Ga..........	170,700	160 Racine, Wis.........	113,500
113 Kalamazoo, Mich.....	170,000	161 Springfield, Ohio.....	112,100
114 Muskegon, Mich......	167,400	162 Manchester, N.H.....	111,900
115 Pensacola, Fla.......	165,400	163 Decatur, Ill.........	111,300
116 Duluth, Minn.– Superior, Wis......	165,200	164 Pueblo, Colo.........	111,000
		165 Springfield, Mo.......	108,700
117 Greenville, S.C.......	164,500	166 Battle Creek, Mich...	107,300
118 Saginaw, Mich.......	160,900	167 Durham, N.C........	106,200
119 Augusta, Ga.........	160,600	168 Green Bay, Wis......	105,300
120 Roanoke, Va.........	160,400	169 Asheville, N.C.......	105,000
121 Utica, N.Y..........	160,400	170 New London, Conn...	104,600
122 Stockton, Calif.......	160,000	171 Altoona, Pa.........	104,500
123 Bakersfield, Calif.....	158,000	172 Newburgh, N.Y......	104,000
124 West Palm Beach, Fla.................	157,200	173 Hamilton, Ohio.......	103,200
		174 Sioux City, Iowa.....	101,500
125 Greensboro, N.C.....	156,800	175 Provo, Utah.........	101,000
126 Montgomery, Ala.*...	155,200	176 High Point, N.C......	100,600
127 Lowell, Mass........	147,400	177 Muncie, Ind.........	100,500
128 York, Pa...........	146,600	178 Petersburg–Hopewell, Va...............	100,300
129 New Bedford, Mass...	146,400	Port Huron, Mich....	62,700
130 Lincoln, Nebr.*......	145,400	*incl. part in Canada.*	124,000
131 Lubbock, Tex........	144,300	Laredo, Tex..........	61,500
132 Portland, Maine......	142,700	*incl. part in Mexico..*	152,500
133 Amarillo, Tex........	142,500	Brownsville, Tex.....	49,500
134 Ogden, Utah.........	141,400	*incl. part in Mexico..*	141,000

a picture as possible of the size and growth of the nation's chief urban centers.

U.S. AIR DISTANCE TABLE

	Albuquerque, N. Mex.	Atlanta, Ga.	Birmingham, Ala.	Boston, Mass.	Buffalo, N.Y.	Burlington, Vt.	Charleston, S.C.	Charlotte, N.C.	Cheyenne, Wyo.	Chicago, Ill.	Cincinnati, Ohio	Cleveland, Ohio	Dallas, Tex.	Denver, Colo.	Detroit, Mich.	Houston, Tex.	Indianapolis, Ind.
Albuquerque, N. Mex......		1272	1138	1972	1580	1878	1539	1457	429	1129	1251	1421	588	334	1364	754	1169
Atlanta, Ga...............	1272		140	937	697	951	267	227	1229	587	369	554	721	1212	596	701	426
Birmingham, Ala..........	1138	140		1052	776	1049	402	361	1119	578	406	618	581	1095	641	567	433
Boston, Mass.............	1972	937	1052		400	182	820	721	1735	851	740	551	1551	1769	613	1605	807
Buffalo, N.Y.............	1580	697	776	400		304	699	538	1335	454	393	173	1198	1370	216	1286	435
Burlington, Vt...........	1878	951	1049	182	304		884	755	1612	749	690	476	1501	1654	516	1580	739
Charleston, S.C..........	1539	267	402	820	699	884		177	1486	757	506	609	981	1474	681	936	594
Charlotte, N.C...........	1457	227	361	721	538	755	177		1362	587	335	435	930	1358	504	927	428
Cheyenne, Wyo............	429	1229	1119	1735	1335	1612	1486	1362		891	1082	1199	726	96	1125	947	986
Chicago, Ill.............	1129	587	578	851	454	749	757	587	891		252	308	803	920	238	940	165
Cincinnati, Ohio.........	1251	369	406	740	393	690	506	335	1082	252		222	814	1094	235	892	100
Cleveland, Ohio..........	1421	554	618	551	173	476	609	435	1199	308	222		1025	1227	90	1114	263
Dallas, Tex..............	588	721	581	1551	1198	1501	981	930	726	803	814	1025		663	999	225	763
Denver, Colo.............	334	1212	1095	1769	1370	1654	1474	1358	96	920	1094	1227	663		1156	879	1000
Detroit, Mich............	1364	596	641	613	216	516	681	504	1125	238	235	90	999	1156		1105	240
Houston, Tex.............	754	701	567	1605	1286	1580	936	927	947	940	892	1114	225	879	1105		865
Indianapolis, Ind........	1169	426	433	807	435	739	594	428	986	165	100	263	763	1000	240	865	
Jacksonville, Fla........	1488	285	374	1017	879	1079	197	341	1493	863	626	770	908	1467	831	821	699
Kansas City, Mo..........	720	676	579	1251	861	1161	928	803	560	414	541	700	451	558	645	644	453
Little Rock, Ark.........	816	456	325	1259	913	1214	723	649	813	552	524	740	293	780	723	388	483
Los Angeles, Calif.......	664	1936	1802	2596	2198	2485	2203	2119	882	1745	1897	2049	1240	831	1983	1374	1809
Louisville, Ky...........	1178	319	331	826	483	780	500	343	1033	269	90	311	726	1038	316	803	107
Memphis, Tenn............	939	337	217	1137	803	1100	604	521	902	482	410	630	420	879	623	484	384
Miami, Fla...............	1698	604	665	1255	1181	1347	482	652	1763	1188	952	1087	1111	1726	1152	968	1024
Minneapolis, Minn........	983	907	862	1123	731	985	1104	939	642	355	605	630	862	700	543	1056	511
New Orleans, La..........	1029	424	312	1359	1086	1361	630	649	1131	833	706	924	443	1082	939	318	712
New York, N.Y............	1815	748	864	188	292	260	641	533	1604	713	570	405	1374	1631	482	1420	646
Omaha, Nebr..............	721	817	732	1282	883	1171	1058	918	463	432	622	739	586	488	669	794	525
Philadelphia, Pa.........	1753	666	783	271	279	328	562	451	1556	666	503	360	1299	1579	443	1341	585
Phoenix, Ariz............	330	1592	1456	2300	1906	2202	1857	1783	663	1453	1581	1749	887	586	1690	1017	1499
Pittsburgh, Pa...........	1499	521	608	483	178	445	528	362	1298	410	257	115	1070	1320	205	1137	330
Portland, Oreg...........	1107	2172	2066	2540	2156	2385	2425	2290	947	1758	1985	2055	1633	982	1969	1836	1885
St. Louis, Mo............	942	467	400	1038	662	966	704	568	795	262	309	492	547	796	455	679	231
Salt Lake City, Utah.....	484	1583	1466	2099	1699	1969	1845	1727	371	1260	1453	1568	999	371	1492	1200	1356
San Antonio, Tex.........	617	882	744	1766	1430	1729	1122	1105	882	1051	1039	1256	252	802	1238	189	999
San Francisco, Calif.....	896	2139	2013	2699	2300	2568	2405	2301	967	1858	2043	2167	1645	949	2091	1645	1949
Seattle, Wash............	1184	2182	2082	2493	2117	2333	2428	2285	973	1737	1972	2026	1681	1021	1938	1891	1872
Tulsa, Okla..............	604	678	552	1398	1023	1327	945	853	588	598	661	853	236	550	813	442	591
Washington, D.C..........	1653	543	661	393	292	432	453	330	1477	597	404	306	1185	1494	396	1220	494
Wichita, Kans............	549	776	658	1424	1036	1337	1039	933	465	591	702	873	340	437	821	559	620

Jacksonville, Fla.	Kansas City, Mo.	Little Rock, Ark.	Los Angeles, Calif.	Louisville, Ky.	Memphis, Tenn.	Miami, Fla.	Minneapolis, Minn.	New Orleans, La.	New York, N.Y.	Omaha, Nebr.	Philadelphia, Pa.	Phoenix, Ariz.	Pittsburgh, Pa.	Portland, Oreg.	St Louis, Mo.	Salt Lake City, Utah	San Antonio, Tex.	San Francisco, Calif.	Seattle, Wash.	Tulsa, Okla.	Washington, D.C.	Wichita, Kans.
1488	720	816	664	1178	939	1698	983	1029	1815	721	1753	330	1499	1107	942	484	617	896	1184	604	1653	549
285	676	456	1936	319	337	604	907	424	748	817	666	1592	521	2172	467	1583	882	2139	2182	678	543	776
374	579	325	1802	331	217	665	862	312	864	732	783	1456	608	2066	400	1466	744	2013	2082	552	661	658
1017	1251	1259	2596	826	1137	1255	1123	1359	188	1282	271	2300	483	2540	1038	2099	1766	2699	2493	1398	393	1424
879	861	913	2198	483	803	1181	731	1086	292	883	279	1906	178	2156	662	1699	1430	2300	2117	1023	292	1036
1079	1161	1214	2485	780	1100	1347	985	1361	260	1171	320	2202	445	2385	966	1969	1729	2568	2333	1327	432	1337
197	928	723	2203	500	604	482	1104	630	641	1058	562	1857	528	2425	704	1845	1122	2405	2428	945	453	1039
341	803	649	2119	343	521	652	939	649	533	918	451	1783	362	2290	568	1727	1105	2301	2285	853	330	933
1493	560	813	882	1033	902	1763	642	1131	1604	463	1556	663	1298	947	795	371	882	967	973	588	1477	465
863	414	552	1745	269	482	1188	355	833	713	432	666	1453	410	1758	262	1260	1051	1858	1737	598	597	591
626	541	524	1897	90	410	952	605	706	570	622	503	1581	257	1985	309	1453	1039	2043	1972	661	404	702
770	740		2049	311	630	1087	630	924	405	739	360	1749	115	2055	492	1568	1256	2166	2026	853	306	873
908	451	293	1240	726	420	1111	862	443	1374	586	1299	887	1070	1633	547	999	252	1483	1681	236	1185	340
1467	558	780	831	1038	879	1726	700	1082	1631	488	1579	586	1320	982	796	371	802	949	1021	550	1494	437
831	645	723	1983	316	623	1152	543	939	482	669	443	1690	205	1969	455	1492	1238	2091	1938	813	396	821
821	644	388	1374	803	484	968	1056	318	1420	794	1341	1017	1137	1836	679	1200	189	1645	1891	442	1220	559
699	453	483	1809	107	384	1024	511	712	646	525	585	1499	330	1885	231	1356	999	1949	1872	591	494	620
	950	690	2147	594	590	326	1191	504	838	1098	758	1794	703	2439	751	1837	1011	2374	2455	921	647	1031
950		325	1356	480	369	1241	413	680	1097	166	1038	1049	781	1497	238	925	702	1506	1506	216	945	177
690	325		1480	435	129	949	708	355	1081	492	1007	1137	779	1759	291	1148	516	1688	1785	231	892	348
2147	1356	1480		1829	1603	2339	1524	1673	2451	1315	2394	357	2136	825	1589	579	1204	347	959	1266	2300	1197
594	480	435	1829		320	919	605	623	652	580	582	1508	344	1950	242	1402	949	1986	1943	582	476	633
590	369	129	1603	320		872	699	358	957	529	881	1263	660	1849	240	1250	631	1802	1867	341	765	442
326	1241	949	2339	919	872		1511	669	1092	1397	1019	1982	1010	2708	1061	2089	1148	2594	2734	1176	923	1297
1191	413	708	1524	605	699	1511		1051	1018	290	985	1280	743	1427	466	987	1110	1584	1395	626	934	546
504	680	355	1673	623	358	669	1051		1171	847	1089	1316	919	2063	598	1434	507	1926	2101	548	966	677
838	1097	1081	2451	652	957	1092	1018	1171		1144	83	2145	317	2445	875	1972	1584	2571	2408	1231	205	1266
1098	166	492	1315	580	529	1397	290	847	1144		1094	1036	836	1371	354	833	828	1429	1369	352	1014	257
758	1038	1007	2394	582	881	1019	985	1089	83	1094		2083	259	2412	811	1925	1507	2523	2380	1163	123	1204
1794	1049	1137	357	1508	1263	1982	1280	1316	2145	1036	2083		1828	1005	1272	504	849	653	1114	932	1983	879
703	781	779	2136	344	660	1010	743	919	317	836	259	1828		2165	559	1668	1291	2264	2138	917	192	950
2439	1497	1759	825	1950	1849	2708	1427	2063	2445	1371	2412	1005	2165		1723	636	1720	534	145	1531	2354	1411
751	238	291	1589	242	240	1061	466	598	875	354	811	1272	559	1723		1162	792	1744	1724	361	712	394
1837	925	1148	579	1402	1250	2089	987	1434	1972	833	1925	504	1668	636	1162		1087	600	701	917	1848	808
1011	702	516	1204	949	631	1148	1110	507	1584	828	1507	849	1291	1720	792	1087		1490	1787	486	1388	573
2374	1506	1688	347	1986	1802	2594	1584	1926	2571	1424	2523	653	2264	534	1744	600	1490		678	1560	2329	1437
2455	1506	1785	959	1943	1867	2734	1395	2101	2408	1369	2380	1114	2138	145	1724	701	1787	678		1560	2329	1437
921	216	231	1266	582	341	1176	626	548	1231	352	1163	932	917	1531	361	917	486	1461	1560		1058	130
647	945	892	2300	476	765	923	934	966	205	1014	123	1983	192	2354	712	1848	1388	2442	2329	1058		1106
1031	177	348	1197	633	442	1297	546	677	1266	257	1204	879	950	1411	394	808	573	1369	1437	130	1106	

GLOSSARY OF MAP TERMINOLOGY

Antarctic Circle. Geographic parallel of 66°33′ S., enclosing area within which the sun is continuously above the horizon on December 22, and below the horizon on June 21.

Arctic Circle. Geographic parallel of 66°33′ N., enclosing area within which the sun is continuously above the horizon on June 21, and below the horizon on December 22.

Continent. One of the main continuous bodies of land on the earth's surface. The number of continents considered to exist varies with usage from five to seven, i. e., America (North and South); Eurasia (Europe and Asia); Africa; Antarctica; and Australia.

Degree. Unit of measurement equal to 1/360 of a circle. A degree of latitude on the earth's surface is roughly equivalent to 69 statute miles. A degree of longitude varies in length but is always equivalent to about 4 minutes of time.

Eastern Hemisphere. Usually considered to be the half of the earth extending from pole to pole between 20° W. and 160° E., including continents of Eurasia, Africa, and Australia.

Equator. Great circle around the earth equidistant from the poles.

Hemisphere. Any half of the earth's surface. See Eastern, Western, and Land Hemisphere.

International Date Line. Line extending from pole to pole along the 180th meridian, with local variations, where each new calendar day begins with the passing of the midnight hour. Travelers crossing the line going west must advance their calendar one day, while those going east must retard calendar one day.

Kilometer. A unit of length; 1,000 meters; 3,280.84 feet; approximately ⅝ of a mile.

Land Hemisphere. The half of earth, centered near Nantes, France, which includes greatest possible land area.

Latitude. The angular distance in degrees of a point on the earth north or south of the Equator.

Longitude. Distance in degrees of a place east or west of Prime Meridian.

Magnetic Declination. From any given place, the angle of magnetic North from true North.

Magnetic Poles. The two locations representing the poles of unlike magnetism belonging to the earth as a magnetized body. The **North Magnetic Pole** is currently located at approximately 73° N. Lat. and 100° W. Long. on Prince of Wales Island. The **South Magnetic Pole** is currently located at approximately 71° S. Lat. and 149° E. Long. in Antarctica.

Map Projection. A network of lines representing parallels of latitude and meridians of longitude, derived by geometrical construction or mathematical analysis.

Map Scale. Relationship which exists between a distance on a map and the corresponding distance on the earth. It may be expressed as an equivalence, one inch equals 16 statute miles; as a fraction or ratio, 1:1,000,000; or as a bar graph sub-divided to show distance which each of its parts represents on the earth.

Meridian. Great circle on earth's surface passing through the poles.

Nautical Mile. A unit commonly used for measuring distances at sea; the length of a minute of latitude; 1,853 meters or 6,080 feet.

Parallels. Small circles on earth's surface, on lines on map, perpendicular to axis of earth and marking latitude north or south of Equator.

Prime Meridian. Meridian on earth's surface from which longitude is measured, generally the meridian of Greenwich, England, on modern maps.

Statute Mile. A unit of distance, 5,280 feet, used in measuring land.

Temperate Zones. The two belts or zones of the earth lying between the Tropics and the Polar Circles.

Torrid Zone. A term formerly used to describe the belt or zone of the earth's surface bounded by Tropic of Cancer and Tropic of Capricorn. Better geographical form today is "Tropical Zone."

Tropic. Line on a map or globe, marking limit reached by overhead or vertical sun in its apparent annual migration. The northern line is called **Tropic of Cancer**, and the southern line **Tropic of Capricorn.** Both are about 23½° from Equator.

Water Hemisphere. That half of the earth centered near New Zealand which includes the greatest possible water area.

Western Hemisphere. Usually considered to be that half of the earth extending from pole to pole between 160° E. and 20° W., thus including the Americas and Greenland.

INDEX

(A gazeteer of political divisions appears on pages 10–27.)

This index includes principal cities in the United States and Canada; capitals of nations, American states, and Canadian provinces; capitals of most of the colonies and dependencies; most great foreign metropolitan centers; and smaller cities and towns of commercial, historical, or cultural significance. Populations are based upon latest available official census figures and estimates.

The index reference key, always a letter and figure combination, and the map page are the last items in each entry. Because some places are shown on both a main map and an inset map, more than one index key may be given for a single map page. Reference also may be made to more than a single map. In each case, however, the index key *letter and figure* precede the map *page number* to which reference is made. A lower-case key letter indicates reference to an inset map which has been keyed separately.

An explanation of how to use the index reference key in finding a place on the map is given on pages 8 and 9.

Aachen, Ger., 143,200........C3 45
Aalborg, Den., 63,909........I3 55
Aalen, Ger., 27,500..........D5 45
Aalst, Bel., 44,179...........B6 43
Aarhus, Den., 113,180.........I4 55
Abadan, Iran, 266,103.........B7 81
Abakan, Sov. Un., 56,000....D12 61
Abbeville, La., 10,414.........D4 131
Abbeville, S.C., 5,436........A3 174
Abeokuta, Nig., 84,000........G5 79
Aberdare, Wales, 40,200......C4 41
Aberdeen, Md., 9,679.........A5 135
Aberdeen, Miss., 6,450.......C5 143
Aberdeen, Scot., 186,400.....B5 39
Aberdeen, S. Dak., 23,073.....D7 165
Aberdeen, Wash., 18,741......C2 185
Abertillery, Wales, 26,800.....C4 41
Abidjan, I. C., 127,585........G4 79
Abilene, Kans., 6,746.........C6 129
Abilene, Tex., 90,368.........C5 179
Abingdon, Ill., 3,469..........C3 125
Abingdon, Va., 4,758..........F3 183
Abington, Mass., 4,500
  (10,607[▲]).................F3 137
Absecon, N.J., 4,320..........E3 155
Acapulco de Juárez, Mex.,
  27,913......................D5 97
Accra, Ghana, 165,000........G4 79
Accrington, Eng., 39,800......A5 41
Acton, Eng., 66,200..........k11 41
Ada, Ohio, 3,918.............C4 167
Ada, Okla., 14,347...........E7 169
Adams, Mass., 12,391.........B1 137
Adana, Tur., 117,799.........D10 59
Addis Ababa, Eth., 129,000...G5 81
Adel, Ga., 4,321.............F2 120
Adelaide, Austl., 75,100
  (*529,000).................F6 85
Aden, Aden, 99,285...........F7 81
Adrano, It., 27,700..........F5 49
Adrian, Mich., 20,347........H7 139
Agawam, Mass., 5,000
  (15,718[▲])................C2 137
Agen, Fr., 33,397............E4 43
Agra, India, 333,530...C6 73, D6 75
Agrigento, It., 35,100........F4 49
Aguascalientes, Mex.,
  93,363..................C4, m12 97
Ahlen, Ger., 34,800..........C3 45
Ahmadabad, India, 788,333
  (*793,813)...........D5 73, F4 75
Ahmadnagar, India, 80,873....E5 73
Ahoskie, N.C., 4,583.........C9 163
Ahwaz, Iran, 45,528..........B7 81

Aiea, Haw., 11,826...........B4 121
Aiken, S.C., 11,243..........B4 174
Aix [-en-Provence], Fr.,
  35,706.....................F6 43
Ajaccio, Fr., 31,434.........D2 49
Ajmer, India,
  196,633..............C5 73, D5 75
Ajo, Ariz., 7,049............E3 107
Akashi, Jap., 120,200........I7 67
Akita, Jap., 190,202.........G10 67
Akmolinsk, Sov. Un.,
  101,000....................D10 61
Akola, India, 89,606.........D6 73
Akron, Ohio, 290,351.........B8 167
Aktyubinsk, Sov. Un., 97,000..D8 61
Akyab, Bur., 42,329..........D7 73
Alameda, Calif., 61,316...E3, B7 113
Alameda, Idaho, 10,660......G7 123
Alamogordo, N. Mex., 21,723..E4 157
Alamo Heights, Tex., 7,552...E2 179
Alamosa, Colo., 6,205........E4 115
Albacete, Sp., 77,239........A7 113
Albany, Calif., 14,804.......E2 113
Albany, Ga., 55,890..........F1 120
Albany, N.Y., 129,726........C7 159
Albany, Oreg., 12,926........C2 171
Albemarle, N.C., 12,261......D5 163
Albert Lea, Minn., 17,108....F5 141
Albertville, Ala., 8,250......B3 105
Albi, Fr., 34,342............F5 43
Albia, Iowa, 4,582...........C5 128
Albion, Mich., 12,749........G7 139
Albion, N.Y., 5,182..........B2 159
Albuquerque, N. Mex.,
  201,189....................B3 157
Alcamo, It., 42,600..........F4 49
Alcázar de San Juan, Sp.,
  25,259.....................C4 47
Alcira, Sp., 25,129..........C5 47
Alcoa, Tenn., 6,395..........B7 175
Alcoy, Sp., 42,454...........C5 47
Aldershot, Eng., 38,700......E6 39
Aleppo (Haleb), Syr., U.A.R.,
  407,613....................D11 59
Alès, Fr., 34,731............E6 43
Alessandria, It., 55,400......B2 49
Alexander City, Ala., 13,140..D4 105
Alexandria (El Iskandarîya), Eg.,
  U.A.R., 1,105,000..........B3 81
Alexandria, Ind., 5,582......C4 127
Alexandria, La., 40,279......B4 131
Alexandria, Minn., 6,713.....D3 141
Alexandria, Va., 91,023......D7 183
Alfortville, Fr., 27,940......g10 43

247

249

257

260

269

New Iberia, La., 29,062......C5 131
New Kensington, Pa., 23,485..C2 173
New Lexington, Ohio, 4,514...E7 167
New London, Conn., 34,182..D7 117
New London, Wis., 5,288.....C5 187
New Malden, Eng., 45,800..m11 39
New Martinsville, W. Va.,
  5,607......................C4 183
Newnan, Ga., 12,169.........D1 120
New Orleans, La., 627,525...D6 131
New Philadelphia, Ohio,
  14,241.....................D9 167
Newport, Ark., 7,007........B6 108
Newport, Eng., 104,900......E5 39
Newport, Ky., 30,070........A6 130
Newport, N.H., 3,222
  (5,458▲)...................E3 153
Newport, Oreg., 5,344.......C1 171
Newport, R.I., 47,049......D11 117
Newport, Tenn., 6,448.......B7 175
Newport, Vt., 5,019.........B3 153
Newport Beach, Calif., 26,564.F6 111
Newport News, Va.,
  113,662.................F8, A7 183
New Richmond, Wis., 3,316...B1 187
New Roads, La., 3,965.......C5 131
New Rochelle, N.Y.,
  76,812.............B4 161, E7 159
New Smyrna, Fla., 8,781.....C8 119
Newton, Iowa, 15,381........C4 128
Newton, Kans., 14,877.......C6 129
Newton, Mass., 92,384...E2, C5 137
Newton, N.J., 6,563..A1 161, A3 155
Newton, N.C., 6,658.........D4 163
Newton Falls, Ohio, 5,038..B10 167
New Toronto, Ont., Can.,
  11,560.....................D3 195
New Ulm, Minn., 11,114......E4 141
New Waterford, N.S., Can.,
  10,381.....................C9 199
New Westminster, B.C., Can.,
  31,665.................D2, D4 191
New York, N.Y.,
  7,781,984..........C4 161, E7 159
Nezhin, Sov. Un., 50,000....F8 57
Niagara Falls, N.Y., 102,394..B2 159
Nice, Fr., 244,360..........F7 43
Nicholasville, Ky., 4,275...B6 130
Nicosia, Cyp., 42,000.......E9 59
Niigata, Jap., 261,758......H9 67
Nijmegen, Neth., 116,989....B6 43
Nikolayev, Sov. Un.,
  224,000.............H9 57, E6 61
Nikopol, Sov. Un., 81,000..H10 57
Niles, Mich., 13,842........H5 139
Niles, Ohio, 19,545........B10 167
Nîmes, Fr., 91,667.........F6 43
Ningpo (Ninghsien), China,
  237,500...................F9 65
Niort, Fr., 32,752.........D3 43
Nipawin, Sask., Can., 3,337..C3 193
Niš, Yugo., 62,100.........D5 51
Niterói, Braz., 255,585....C4, h6 89
Nitro, W. Va., 6,894.......D3 183
Nizhniy Tagil, Sov. Un.,
  338,000...................D9 61
Nkana, Rh. & Nya., 27,500...C5 83
Nobeoka, Jap., 116,762......J5 67
Noblesville, Ind., 7,664....C3 127
Nogales, Ariz., 7,286......F5 107
Nogales, Mex., 24,480......A2 97
Nōgata, Jap., 62,520.......J5 67
Noginsk, Sov. Un.,
  93,000.........D12, n18 57, D6 61

Noorvik, Alsk., 329.........B7 104
Norco, Calif., 4,964........C5 109
Nordenham, Ger., 27,200.....B4 45
Nordhausen, Ger., 32,848....C5 45
Nordhorn, Ger., 37,100......B3 45
Norfolk, Nebr., 13,640......C8 149
Norfolk, Va., 305,872....F8, A8 183
Norilsk, Sov. Un., 108,000..C11 61
Normal, Ill., 13,357........C5 125
Norman, Okla., 33,412.......D6 169
Norristown, Pa., 38,925.....C6 173
Norrköping, Swe.,
  88,769................u34, H7 55
North Abington, Mass., 4,900.F3 137
North Adams, Mass., 19,905..B1 137
Northampton, Eng., 101,800..D6 39
Northampton, Mass., 30,058..C2 137
North Attleboro, Mass.,
  14,777.....................D5 137
North Battleford, Sask., Can.,
  8,924......................C2 193
North Bay, Ont., Can.,
  21,020.....................C5 195
North Bend, Oreg., 7,512....D1 171
North Braddock, Pa., 13,204..A4 173
North Canton, Ohio, 7,727...C9 167
North Charleston, S.C.,
  22,339.....................C6 174
North Chicago, Ill.,
  20,517.............A2 126, A6 125
North Dartmouth, Mass.,
  4,000......................D5 137
North East, Pa., 4,217......A2 173
Northfield, Minn., 8,707....E5 141
North Kingstown, R.I.,
  10,000...................C10 117
North Little Rock, Ark.,
  58,032.....................C5 108
North Manchester, Ind.,
  4,377......................C4 127
North Pelham, N.Y., 5,326...B4 161
North Plainfield, N.J., 16,993.B4 155
North Platte, Nebr., 17,184..D5 149
Northport, Ala., 5,245......C2 105
Northport, N.Y., 5,972......B6 161
North Providence, R.I.,
  18,220...................B10 117
North St. Paul, Minn., 8,520..C8 141
North Sydney, N.S., Can.,
  8,125......................C9 199
North Tarrytown, N.Y.,
  8,818......................A4 161
North Tonawanda, N.Y.,
  34,757.....................B2 159
Northumberland, Pa., 4,156..C5 173
North Vancouver, B.C., Can.,
  19,951................D2, D4 191
North Vernon, Ind., 4,062...D4 127
Northville, Mich., 3,967....B7 139
North Wilkesboro, N.C.,
  4,197......................C4 163
Norton, Kans., 3,345........B4 129
Norton, Va., 4,996.........F2 183
Novi, Mich., 6,390.........B7 139
Norwolk, Calif., 88,739.....C3 109
Norwalk, Conn.,
  67,775.............A6 161, E2 117
Norwalk, Ohio, 12,900.......B6 167
Norwich, Conn., 38,506......C7 117
Norwich, Eng., 120,300......D7 39
Norwich, N.Y., 9,175........C5 159
Norwood, Mass.,
  24,898................E2, C5 137
Norwood, Ohio, 34,580.......F3 167

278

Paxton, Ill., 4,370..........C5 125
Payette, Idaho, 4,451......E3 123
Paysandú, Ur., 65,000.......E1 89
Payson, Utah, 4,237........C4 181
Pazardzhik, Bul., 39,520.....D7 51
Peabody, Mass., 32,202.....D3 137
Pearsall, Tex., 4,957.......E5 179
Pecos, Tex., 12,728........D3 179
Pécs, Hung., 110,000........B4 51
Peekskill, N.Y., 18,737.....D7 159
Peine, Ger., 27,900........B5 45
Pekalongan, Indon., 55,406...G3 69
Pekin, Ill., 28,146.........C4 125
Peking (Peiping), China,
    4,010,000................D8 65
Pelham, Ga., 4,609.........F1 120
Pella, Iowa, 5,198.........C5 128
Pelotas, Braz., 78,014.......E2 89
Pembroke, Ont., Can., 15,434.C5 195
Penang, Mala., 234,855.....J4 71
Pen Argyl, Pa., 3,671......C6 173
Peñarroya-Pueblonuevo, Sp.,
    27,728..................C3 47
Penbrook, Pa., 3,671.......C5 173
Pendleton, Oreg., 14,434....B7 171
Penki, China, 449,000......C9 65
Pennsauken, N.J., 33,771....D2 155
Penns Grove, N.J., 6,176....D2 155
Penn Yan, N.Y., 5,770......C3 159
Pensacola, Fla., 56,752.....B1 119
Penza, Sov. Un.,
    254,000........E15 57, D7 61
Peoria, Ill., 103,162........C4 125
Pergamino, Arg., 32,382.....A4 91
Périgueux, Fr., 40,865......E4 43
Perkasie, Pa., 4,650........C6 173
Perovo, Sov. Un., 143,000...n17 57
Perpignan, Fr., 74,984......F5 43
Perry, Fla., 8,030.........B5 119
Perry, Ga., 6,032..........E2 120
Perry, Iowa, 6,442.........C3 128
Perry, N.Y., 4,629.........C2 159
Perry, Okla., 5,210........C6 169
Perrysburg, Ohio, 5,519.....A4 167
Perryton, Tex., 7,903.......A4 179
Perryville, Mo., 5,117......D7 145
Perth, Austl., 119,320
    (*376,000)...............F2 85
Perth, Scot., 41,100........B5 39
Perth Amboy, N.J.,
    38,007..........C2 161, B4 155
Peru, Ill., 10,460.........B4 125
Peru, Ind., 14,453.........C3 127
Perugia, It., 41,500........C4 49
Pervouralsk, Sov. Un.,
    90,000..................D8 61
Pesaro, It., 35,900........C4 49
Pescara, It., 71,500.......C5 49
Pestszenterzsebet, Hung.,
    70,072..................B4 51
Petaluma, Calif., 14,035....D3 113
Peterborough, Ont., Can.,
    42,698..................D5 195
Peterborough, Eng., 54,400..D6 39
Petersburg, Alsk., 1,502.g17,D13 104
Petersburg, Va., 36,750.....E7 183
Petoskey, Mich., 6,138......D7 139
Petropavlovsk, Sov. Un.,
    131,000.................D9 61
Petropavlovsk [-Kamchatskiy],
    Sov. Un., 86,000.........D18 61
Petrópolis, Braz., 61,011...C4, n6 89
Petrovgrad, Yugo., 32,838....C5 51

Petrovsk [-Zabaykalskiy], Sov.
    Un., 59,000..............D13 61
Petrozavodsk, Sov. Un.,
    135,000.........A10 57, C6 61
Pforzheim, Ger., 62,000.....D4 45
Phenix City, Ala., 27,630....D4 105
Philadelphia, Miss., 5,017...D4 143
Philadelphia, Pa.,
    2,002,512........A6, D6 173
Philipsburg, Pa., 3,872.....C3 173
Phillipsburg, Kans., 3,233...B4 129
Phillipsburg, N.J., 18,502...B2 155
Phoenix, Ariz., 439,170.....D3 107
Phoenixville, Pa., 13,797....C6 173
Phom Penh, Camb., 123,883..G6 71
Piacenza, It., 62,400.......B2 49
Piatra-Neamt, Rom., 32,648..B8 51
Piazza Armerina, It., 27,900.F5 49
Picayune, Miss., 7,834......F4 143
Pictou, N.S., Can., 4,564....D7 199
Piedmont, Ala., 4,794.......C4 105
Piedmont, Calif., 11,117....A7 113
Piedras Negras, Mex., 27,578.B4 97
Pierre, S. Dak., 10,088.....E5 165
Pietermaritzburg, S. Afr.,
    73,273..................F6 83
Pikeville, Ky., 4,754.......B8 130
Pikesville, Md., 18,737.....C2 135
Pine Bluff, Ark., 44,037....C5 108
Pineville, La., 8,636.......B4 131
Pinole, Calif., 6,064.......A7 113
Piombino, It., 28,700.......C3 49
Piotrkow [Trybunalski], Pol.,
    48,000..................C5 53
Pipestone, Minn., 5,324.....E2 141
Piqua, Ohio, 19,219........D3 167
Piracicaba, Braz., 45,782..C3, m8 89
Piraievs (Piraeus), Grc.,
    186,014.................D4 59
Pirmasens, Ger., 48,800.....D3 45
Pirna, Ger., 37,426........C6 45
Pisa, It., 81,100..........C3 49
Pistoia, It., 34,100.......C3 49
Pitcairn, Pa., 5,383.......A4 173
Pitești, Rom., 38,333......C7 51
Pitman, N.J., 8,644........D2 155
Pittsburg, Calif., 19,062..A9, D4 113
Pittsburg, Kans., 18,678....D9 129
Pittsburg, Pa., 604,332....A4, C1 173
Pittsburg, Tex., 3,796......B5 177
Pittsfield, Ill., 4,089......D3 125
Pittsfield, Maine, 3,232
    (4,010^A)................D2 132
Pittsfield, Mass., 57,879....C1 137
Pittston, Pa., 12,407....A5, B6 173
Placentia, Calif., 5,861....C4 109
Placerville, Calif., 4,439...D5 113
Plainfield, N.J.,
    45,330..........C2 161, B4 155
Plainview, N.Y., 27,710.....B6 161
Plainview, Tex., 18,735.....B4 179
Plano, Tex., 3,695.........B4 177
Plant City, Fla., 15,711....D6 119
Plaquemine, La., 7,689......C5 131
Platteville, Wis., 6,957....E3 187
Plattsburg, N.Y., 20,172....A7 159
Plattsmouth, Nebr., 6,244...E10 149
Plauen, Ger., 84,778.......C6 45
Pleasant Hill, Calif., 23,844..A8 113
Pleasanton, Tex., 3,467.....E5 179
Pleasant Ridge, Mich., 3,807.B8 139
Pleasantville, N.J., 15,172..E3 155
Pleasantville, N.Y., 5,877...A4 161
Pleven, Bul., 57,758........D7 51

279

282

285

Stuttgart, Ger., 566,000
(*750,000)..............D4 45
Subotica, Yugo., 115,342....B4 51
Succasunna, N.J., 2,500.....B1 161
Suchow, China, 340,000......E8 65
Sucre, Bol., 40,128.........E4 87
Sudbury, Ont., Can., 46,482..C4 195
Sueca, Sp., 20,409..........C5 47
Suez, Eg., U.A.R., 115,000...C4 81
Suffern, N.Y., 5,094........A3 161
Suffolk, Va., 12,609.....F8, B7 183
Suitland, Md., 10,300.......C2 135
Sukkur, Pak., 77,057........C4 73
Sullana, Peru, 26,330.......D2 87
Sullivan, Ill., 3,946.......D5 125
Sullivan, Ind., 4,979.......D2 127
Sullivan, Mo., 4,098........C5 145
Sulphur, Okla., 4,737.......E7 169
Sulphur Springs, Tex., 9,160..B5 177
Summerside, P.E.I., Can.,
  7,242....................C6 199
Summerville, S.C., 3,633....C5 174
Summit, Ill., 10,374........C2 126
Summit, N.J., 23,677.C2 161, B4 155
Summit Hill, Pa., 4,386.....C6 173
Sumter, S.C., 23,062........B5 174
Sunbury, Pa., 13,687........C5 173
Sunchŏn, Kor., 61,647.......I3 67
Suncook, N.H., 3,807........E5 153
Sundbyberg, Swe., 24,098....t35 55
Sunderland, Eng., 182,800...C6 39
Sundsvall, Swe., 27,674.....F7 55
Sungchiang, China, 67,000...E9 65
Sunnyside, Wash., 6,208.....C5 185
Sunnyvale, Calif., 52,898...C8 113
Sun Prairie, Wis., 4,008....D4 187
Superior, Ariz., 4,875......D4 107
Superior, Nebr., 2,935......E7 149
Superior, Wis., 33,563......A1 187
Surabaja, Indon., 935,700...G4 69
Surakarta, Indon., 369,800..G4 69
Surat, India, 223,182.D5 73, G4 75
Surbiton, Eng., 62,600......m11 39
Suresnes, Fr., 32,182.......g9 43
Susanville, Calif., 5,598...B5 113
Sussex, N.B., Can., 3,403...D4 199
Sutton [& Cheam], Eng.,
  78,800...................m12 39
Sutton Coldfield, Eng.,
  52,510...................B6 41
Sutton-in-Ashfield, Eng.,
  40,300...................D6 39
Suzuka, Jap., 80,741........o15 67
Sverdlovsk, Sov. Un.,
  770,000..............q22 57, D9 61
Svobodnyy, Sov. Un.,
  57,000...................D15 61
Swainsboro, Ga., 5,943......E3 120
Swampscott, Mass.,
  13,294..............D3, C6 137
Swan River, Man., Can.,
  2,644....................C3 193
Swansea, Ont., Can., 8,595..D3 195
Swansea, Wales, 161,700.....C4 41
Swanton, Ohio, 2,306........A4 167
Swanton, Vt., 2,390
  (3,946ᴬ).................B1 153
Swarthmore, Pa., 5,753......A6 173
Swatow, China, 280,400......G8 65
Sweetwater, Tenn., 4,145....B6 175
Sweetwater, Tex., 13,914....C4 179
Swidnica, Pol., 34,000......C4 53
Swietochlowice, Pol., 56,500..g9 53

Swift Current, Sask., Can.,
  10,612...................C2 193
Swindon, Eng., 74,000.......E6 39
Swoyersville, Pa., 6,751...A5, B6 173
Sycamore, Ill., 6,961.......A5 125
Sydney, Austl., 230,330
  (*1,975,020).............F9 85
Sydney, N.S., Can., 32,162..C9 199
Sydney Mines, N.S., Can.,
  8,731....................C9 199
Sylacauga, Ala., 12, 857....C3 105
Sylvania, Ga., 3,469........E4 120
Sylvester, Ga., 3,610.......F2 120
Syracuse, N.Y., 216,038.....B4 159
Syzran, Sov. Un., 148,000...D7 61
Szczecin (Stettin), Pol.,
  223,000..................B3 53
Szeged, Hung., 100,000......B5 51
Székesfehérvár, Hung.,
  52,000...................B4 51
Szentes, Hung., 26,000......B5 51
Szeping, China, 76,000......C9 65
Szolnok, Hung., 43,000......B5 51
Szombathely, Hung., 53,000..B3 51

Taber, Alta., Can., 3,688...D6 191
Tabriz, Iran, 290,195.......A7 81
Tachikawa, Jap., 63,644.....n18 67
Tacoma, Wash., 147,979......B3 185
Taegu (Taikyū), Kor.,
  488,690..................I4 67
Taejŏn, Kor., 173,143.......H3 67
Taft, Calif., 3,822.........D4 111
Taganrog, Sov. Un., 201,000.H12 57
Tahlequah, Okla., 5,840.....D9 169
Taichung, For., 199,519.....G9 65
Tainan, For., 221,088.......G9 65
Taipei, For., 503,086.......G9 65
Taiyuan, China, 252,000.....D7 65
Takamatsu, Jap., 144,812....I7 67
Takaoka, Jap., 131,531......H8 67
Takasaki, Jap.,
  125,195.............m18, H9 67
Takoma Park, Md., 16,799....C1 135
Talavera de la Reina, Sp.,
  21,728...................B2 47
Talca, Chile, 55,059........B2 91
Talcahuano, Chile, 54,782...B2 91
Talladega, Ala., 17,742.....C3 105
Tallahassee, Fla., 48,174...B4 119
Tallassee, Ala., 4,934......D4 105
Tallinn, Sov. Un.,
  280,000............B5 57, D5 61
Tallmadge, Ohio, 10,246.....B9 167
Tallulah, La., 9,413........A5 131
Tama, Iowa, 2,925...........C5 128
Tamaqua, Pa., 10,173........C6 173
Tambov, Sov. Un., 170,000
  (*190,000)..........E3 57, D7 61
Tampa, Fla., 274,970........E6 119
Tampere, Fin., 95,753.......G10 55
Tampico, Mex.,
  94,342..............C5, k15 97
Tananarive, Malag., 174,200
  (*245,000)...............D9 83
Tandil, Arg., 32,309........B5 91
Tangier, Mor., 100,000......A3 79
Tanjore, India, 100,680.....F6 73
Tanta, Eg., U.A.R., 151,700..B4 81
Taos, N. Mex., 2,163........A4 157
Tapachula, Mex., 30,027.....E6 97
Tarabulus (Tripoli), Leb.,
  109,000..................E10 59
Taranto, It., 180,500.......D6 49

288

289

294

Woodstock, Ont., Can.,
18,347.....................D4 195
Woodstock, Ill., 8,897........A5 125
Woodstock, Va., 2,083........D6 183
Woodstown, N.J., 2,942........D2 155
Woodward, Okla., 7,747......C4 169
Woolwich, Eng., 127,500....m13 39
Woonsocket, R.I., 47,080......A9 117
Wooster, Ohio, 17,046.......C8 167
Worcester, Eng., 63,400......D5 39
Worcester, Mass., 186,587....C4 137
Workington, Eng., 29,100....C5 39
Worksop, Eng., 33,800.......A6 41
Worland, Wyo., 5,806........B5 189
World, 2,666,000,000.......... 35
Worms, Ger., 57,200.........D4 45
Worth, Ill., 8,196...........D2 126
Worthing, Eng., 71,600.......E6 39
Worthington, Minn., 9,015...F3 141
Worthington, Ohio, 9,239....D6 167
Wŏsan (Gensan), Kor.,
112,952.....................G3 67
Wrangell, Alsk.,
1,315...............g17, D13 104
Wray, Colo., 2,082...........B7 115
Wrexham, Wales, 32,800.....A5 41
Wrightsville, Ga., 2,056......E3 120
Wroclaw (Breslau), Pol.,
374,000....................C4 53
Wuchin, China, 80,000.......E8 65
Wuchow, China, 110,800.....G7 65
Wuhan, China, 2,146,000.....E7 65
Wuhu, China, 242,100.......E8 65
Wuppertal, Ger., 392,800.....C3 45
Würzburg, Ger., 94,200......D4 45
Wusih, China, 581,500.......E9 65
Wyandotte, Mich., 43,519....C8 139
Wynne, Ark., 4,922..........B7 108
Wynne Wood, Okla., 2,509...E6 169
Wyoming, Pa., 4,127.........A4 173
Wytheville, Va., 5,634.......F3 183

Xanthi, Grc., 25,700.........B5 59
Xenia, Ohio, 20,445..........E4 167

Yakima, Wash., 43,284......C5 185
Yakutsk, Sov. Un., 74,000...C15 61
Yalta, Sov. Un., 47,100......I10 57
Yamagata, Jap., 160,245....G10 67
Yamaguchi, Jap., 81,177.....I5 67
Yambol, Bul., 42,038.........D8 51
Yangchow, China, 127,000....E8 65
Yankton, S. Dak., 9,279......G8 165
Yaoundé, Cam., 55,000......H7 79
Yarkand, China, 80,000......F10 63
Yarmouth, N.S., Can., 8,095..F3 199
Yaroslavl, Sov. Un.,
406,000...........C12 57, D6 61
Yates Center, Kans., 2,080...D8 129
Yawata, Jap., 286,241........J5 67
Yawatahama, Jap., 55,471....J6 67
Yazoo City, Miss., 11,236....D3 143
Yecla, Sp., 21,257...........C5 47
Yegoryevsk, Sov. Un.,
59,000..............D12, n19 57
Yelets, Sov. Un.,
78,000............E12 57, D6 61
Yellow Springs, Ohio, 4,167...E4 167

Yenakiyevo, Sov. Un.,
92,000............G12, q21 57
Yeovil, Eng., 24,000.........E5 39
Yerevan, Sov. Un., 509,000...E7 61
Yingkow, China, 131,400.....C9 65
Yoakum, Tex., 5,761.........D4 177
Yokkaichi, Jap.,
170,602.................o15, I8 67
Yokohama, Jap.,
1,143,687................n18, I9 67
Yokosuka, Jap., 279,132..n18, I9 67
Yonago, Jap., 90,024.........I6 67
Yonezawa, Jap., 95,714.....H10 67
Yonkers, N.Y.,
190,634.........B4 161, E7 159
York, Ala., 2,932............D1 105
York, Eng., 106,200.........D6 39
York, Nebr., 6,173...........E8 149
York, Pa., 54,504............D5 173
York, S.C., 4,758............A4 174
Yorkton, Sask., Can., 8,256...C3 193
Yorktown, Tex., 2,527.......D4 177
Youngstown, Ohio, 166,689..B10 167
Ypsilanti, Mich., 20,957......G8 139
Yreka, Calif., 4,759..........A3 113
Yuba City, Calif., 11,507.....C4 113
Yuma, Ariz., 23,974.........E1 107
Yungning, China, 203,000....G6 65
Yuzhno-Sakhalinsk, Sov. Un.,
86,000.....................E17 61

Zabrze, Pol.,
182,000................C5, g9 53
Zagreb, Yugo., 350,829......C2 51
Zagazig, Eg., U.A.R.,
81,813.....................B4 81
Zamora, Sp., 35,392.........B3 47
Zamosc, Pol., 26,000.........C7 53
Zanesville, Ohio, 39,077.....E7 167
Zanzibar, Zan., 45,276.......B7 83
Zapata, Tex., 2,031..........E3 177
Zaporozhye, Sov. Un.,
435,000.........H10 57, E6 61
Zaragoza, Sp., 282,394......B5 47
Zawiercie, Pol., 31,000...C5, g10 53
Zeist, Neth., 46,634.........A6 43
Zeitz, Ger., 39,581..........C6 45
Zemun, Yugo., 28,083.......C5 51
Zenica, Yugo., 30,000.......C3 51
Zgierz, Pol., 32,000.........C5 53
Zhdanov (Mariupol), Sov. Un.,
284,000.........H11 57, E6 61
Zhitomir, Sov. Un.,
105,000...........F7 57, D5 61
Zion, Ill., 11,941...........A5 125
Zittau, Ger., 45,084.........C7 45
Zlatoust, Sov. Un., 161,000..D8 61
Zonguldak, Tur., 35,631.....B8 59
Zrenjanin (Petrovgrad), Yugo.,
45,300....................C5 51
Zürich, Switz., 409,300
(*438,300)................E4 45
Zutphen, Neth., 23,793......A7 43
Zweibrücken, Ger., 30,000....D3 45
Zwickau, Ger., 122,862......C6 45
Zwolle, Neth., 52,455........A7 43
Zyrardow, Pol., 27,000..B6, m12 53

Rand McNally

WORLD ATLASES

INTERNATIONAL WORLD ATLAS

An outstanding new atlas with beautiful up
date color maps giving a complete picture
the entire world. Many detailed maps of Af
show latest developments on new countries
comprehensive index to more than 80,000 ple
contains final 1960 census figures for the u
States. 136 pages are devoted to detailed m
Geographical and historical information is c
tained in tables on U. S. Metropolitan Are
Census, World Cities, Mountains and Riv
Historical Gazetteer, etc.

312 pages; 11¼ x 14¼ inches; buckram bindi

$11.9

COLLEGIATE WORLD ATLAS

This new handy-size World Atlas is designed for
the entire family. 178 pages of full color political maps and 33 pages of full color historical
maps covering the entire world make this Atlas
especially valuable to the student. A comprehensive index to more than 25,000 places gives final
1960 census figures for U. S. cities. 120 pages of
up-to-date factual information about countries,
cities, climates, economies, history, geographical
relationships, universities, colleges, round out
this distinctive and practical reference atlas.
7⅜ x 10¾ inches; 416 pages; cloth bound.

$6.95

READERS WORLD ATLAS

This brand new census edition in its "easy-t
handle" size is an exceptional value in a "good
atlas. Final census figures for U. S. cities a
featured in this up-to-date index of more tho
25,000 places. Latest political changes are show
in 178 pages of beautiful full-color maps whic
cover the world in detail. Individual maps o
nearly every state and Canadian province mak
this an outstanding reference atlas.
7⅜ x 10¾ inches; 300 pages; cloth bound.

$4.9